WALKING THE PATH OF LOVE

Lessons on living.

Joseph J. Mazzella

xulon
PRESS

Copyright © 2010 by Joseph J. Mazzella

Walking The Path Of Love
Lessons on living.
by Joseph J. Mazzella

Printed in the United States of America

ISBN 9781609573775

All rights reserved solely by the author. The author guarantees all contents are original and do not infringe upon the legal rights of any other person or work. No part of this book may be reproduced in any form without the permission of the author. The views expressed in this book are not necessarily those of the publisher.

www.xulonpress.com

INTRODUCTION

I would have never thought twenty plus years ago when I wrote my first inspirational "article" that I would still be doing it today. At the time it was just a way to share a bit of joy and truth that I'd discovered. Thankfully, the editor of my local county newspaper was kind enough to publish it for me. That then led to another article and another, week after week, until now the 19 year old boy who wrote them is a 43 year old man.

Over that time other local papers have published my work and with the rise of the internet, I found a world wide family to share them with as well. I can't thank enough all of the newspaper and website editors who shared my work with their readers. Without them my words would have had no wings and would never have flown across this globe to touch all the souls they have.

One question I have been asked over these many years of writing these uplifting essays is: "When are you going to write a book?" For one reason or another the time or circumstances has never been right until now. That is why I am happy to finally be able to share this collection of some of my favorite writings.

I titled this book: WALKING THE PATH OF LOVE because in one way or another that is what I have been doing for most of my life. In fact, that is what most of us have been doing whether we realize it or not.

These articles aren't presented in chronological order. Each one is a moment taken from my life. Whether it is an idea I had, a memory that warmed my heart, or an experience that kept me walking on the path each article has its own distinct truth and can stand on its own.

In these writings you will follow my life through its ups and downs, struggles and triumphs, sadness and joy. You will share in what I learned, how I grew, and who I became. I don't claim credit for the thoughts and truths presented here. I am not that wise a man or gifted a writer. I instead allowed God to teach me and write through me so I could share it all with you.

The themes and pieces of wisdom on these pages come from Heaven itself and are as varied as life itself. If I tried to explain them all in this introduction then I would be writing a whole other book.

There are four main points, however, that I find myself making over in over in my writings. Perhaps it is because I am still fully learning them myself. It is these four points that I want you to keep in mind as you read this book. I hope that you will welcome their truth into your mind, heart, and soul. I hope that you will make them a part of your life as well. It can make the difference between a life well lived or a life well wasted. It can make the difference between a happy and helpful existence in this world or a despairing and desperate one.

1. GOD LOVES YOU

Yes, it is true whether you wish to believe it or not. God loves you with a love beyond anything you can imagine. God's love is endless, eternal, and unconditional. It is powerful and brings a peace beyond all understanding. It is joyous and brings hope and happiness to every heart willing to accept it. God's love is everywhere and in each one of us.

God is ready to manifest His love in your life too if you let him. You will see how many different ways it was manifested in mine in the articles I have written over the years. It has come in people, experiences, nature, music, books, animals, dreams, intuition, thoughts, feelings, and actions. Over all of my life God's love for me has been constant, perfect, and waiting. It has just taken me a long time to fully accept it into my life and welcome it into my heart. When I did, however, the joy that followed has been beyond my ability to describe. I can only hint at it in these writings to you and pray that you welcome it into your life as well.

2. YOU CAN CHOOSE LOVE TOO.

This may be the thing I have written most about over the years. Too many people think that love and life are things that happen to them. They think that only by having the outside world right will they finally be happy. What I have learned more than anything else over the years and what I am still learning today is that love is a choice we make. I am not just talking about romantic love either. I am talking about love of life, love of ourselves, love for this world and everyone in it, and most importantly love of God. If you can start choosing love moment by moment and day by day then your life will begin to change in ways you never thought could be possible. You will be walking the path and you will be meeting fellow travelers along the way. Your journey will become blessed and you will see that you are not only on your way to Heaven but that you are also bringing Heaven to Earth with every step you take.

Choosing to love will give you everything you ever needed but didn't realize you needed. It will make the pleasures of fame, fortune, and success seem hollow by comparison. It will teach you what life is all about and move you to teach others as well. It will turn your life into a wonderful adventure of doing good, being kind, and helping others. Your sadness will be replaced with smiles and your depression will become delight. You will be living the way you were meant to live and being who you were meant to be: A CHILD OF GOD.

3. WHEN YOU LOVE YOU WILL HAVE JOY

This one is the key to everything I wanted to learn in life and that is why I am so delighted to share it in all my writings. You see, we all want to be happy. We all want JOY. It doesn't matter what we list as our dreams or goals, their purpose is always to lead us to joy. Some of us thank that comes from a successful career, or the right relationship, or the perfect family, or even winning the lottery. The truth is that none of those things can bring you lasting joy. Lasting joy only comes when you love. When you love, LIFE IS JOY. You see, God created us to share in His love. He created us to love each other. When we do so then we receive the ultimate gift that we wall wish for: joy. We were created in love. We were created by Love for "God is love". When we love God, ourselves, and each other then joy naturally follows. Choosing love, sharing love, learning of love, growing in love, and becoming one with God's love is what we were all sent here to do. It is the meaning of life. It is the path to eternal life. And it is what makes for a joyous journey.

4. EVEN THE PAIN, SUFFERING, AND TRAGEDIES WE GO THROUGH CAN LEAD US TO GREATER LEARNING, LOVE, AND JOY.

This might be the hardest truth for many of you to accept. It certainly was the hardest truth for me to accept. I wanted the easy life with lots of money, success, and good things. I wanted happy relationships and no pain, thank you very much. Well, that is not how life works. We have to know suffering to know joy. We have to experience pain to fully experience love. We have to face loss to gain faith. God knows that we are going through all these things, but He also knows that they are temporary. In the eyes of eternity our lives here are but an instant. We all too often waste that instant on foolish pursuits, though. It is pain, suffering, and loss that wakes us up from our selfishness and reminds us of what is important in life. Ask any cancer survivor what they have learned and they will tell you that facing cancer showed them just how precious life and love are. I know that losing my own Mother when I was only 25 years old made me see that I can't waste a moment because life here can be over in a moment. If I want to love, I have to love now. I know having two mentally handicapped sons brought me so much pain and frustration over the years. Yet, it has taught me a depth of love, patience, and compassion that I could never have achieved without the lessons they gave me. As I hug them and tell them I love them everyday, I also thank God for giving them to me. They helped me become who I am today. They led me back to God's love, helped me to see that I can choose love as well, and allowed me to find joy everyday of my life. It is true that God in His loving wisdom can use all things for the good of those who love Him.

As you read the pages that follow keep in mind these 4 truths. Allow them to flow into your heart and fill your soul. Allow them to become part of your life and part of who you are. Then go out and share them with the world. If this book inspires one beautiful soul out there to do one more loving act of kindness then every word I have written over the last 24 years will have been worth it. God bless you always. Know that I am wishing you every joy.

Joseph Mazzella

I have learned that it doesn't matter how many times you stumble and fall. It only matters how many time you get back up.

WALKING THE PATH

Growing up in these rugged mountains of West Virginia I have had the joy of walking many trails and paths over the years. There have been ones that went across sun-drenched meadows and there have been ones that went through shady woods. There have been ones next to roaring rivers and there have been ones next to peaceful lakes. There have been ones going uphill and there have been ones going downhill. There have been smooth, grassy ones and there have been ones full of rocks and holes. Still, each one has had its own special delight. I have loved walking along them all too even though I have stumbled and fallen a few times.

When it comes to the path of my life, however, I have stumbled and fallen more than just a few times. Actually, I have hit the ground more times than I can count. It hasn't always been a grassy trail over a sun-drenched meadow for me. It has been a path full of twists, turns, rocks, holes, and obstacles as well. I haven't always kept my eyes on the road or my hand in God's either. Still, no matter how many times I have ended up face down in the dirt God has always been there to forgive me and help me back up. I have learned too that it doesn't matter how many times you stumble and fall. It only matters how many times you get back up. Even if you stumble and fall one million times then you need to rise up and try again one million and one. God is always there waiting to forgive you and help you to walk your life's path one more time.

I can see too now why God sent me along this path my life has taken. It lead me to where I am now. Without the growth it gave, learning it provided, and even falls it dealt me I would not be who I am today. I plan on continuing down my life's path then doing all the good I can and helping others along the way. I plan on walking it with a smile on my face, a song on my lips, love in my heart, joy in my soul, and my hand firmly in God's. I know it is leading me home.

Each of us has our own song to sing in this life.

A CHORUS OF JOY

When I went outside this morning I was greeted with something that I hadn't heard in a long time. It was the sweet music of birdsong and it lifted my heart in joy to hear it again. I had missed that beautiful music all through the Winter and hearing it now welcoming the coming Spring filled me with delight. There were dozens of different birds each singing their own individual songs and yet they blended together perfectly. They sung of love, joy, and rebirth. They sung of beauty, happiness, and light. They sung of goodness, glory, and oneness with God. It was a concert that brought peace to the soul and happiness to the mind. I felt so blessed to be able to hear it.

Sometimes I think that we are like those birds who greeted the morning with such zest and bliss. Each of us is different. Each of us has our own song to sing in this life. Still, when we go deep enough into our souls we see that the source of all our songs is the same. It is the love, joy, and light within us that is our music. It is our music that we must share with the world. Our music is our gift from God and the song we choose to sing is our gift to each other. They may all be different, but they come from the same love, joy, and God. They may all be unique but they blend together perfectly.

Don't be afraid to sing your song then. Don't be afraid to share the music that is within you right now. Your song may not be what the rest of the world sings, but God will see to it that it blends together wonderfully with the others to create a chorus of love and joy. Let your music out and bless this world with the unique song that you have been given. I know that the world will delight in hearing it.

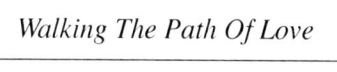

God blesses the world with Spring once a year but blesses us with Spring everyday of our lives.

EMBRACING SPRING

After a long, cold, and rough Winter I am patiently counting the days now until Spring arrives here in the mountains of my home. It will be so glorious to see the rebirth of the world once again. Soon the first dandelion will cautiously poke its head through the ground to delight in the newly warm air. Soon the Apple, Dogwood, and Cherry trees will awaken and fill their limbs with brilliant and fragrant blossoms. Soon the mountains will turn a thousand shades of green as the leaves appear and every glance at them will bring a smile to my face. Soon the meadows will be full of fresh, new grass that will an inviting carpet for any barefoot child to walk on. Soon the skies will be full of returning birds and their Heavenly songs will make my heart sing as well. Soon the gentle breezes will carry the dance of the butterflies as they float happily from flower to flower. Soon the beautiful sounds of talking neighbors, laughing teenagers, and playing children will fill the air as everyone ventures out to enjoy the mild temperatures and golden sunshine.

When those days get here I will embrace them with all of my heart, soul, and mind. I will look to the Heavens as well and thank God for once again bringing new life to this world. Most of all, though, I will seek out the Springtime within myself and continue to share it with everyone I meet.

You see, God blesses the world with Spring once a year but blesses us with Spring everyday of our lives. Each time we pray, share our love, spread our joy, stop to help another, or do a single act of kindness it is once again Springtime in our souls. Embrace the Springtime in within you then no matter what the season. Live from the eternal Spring of life, goodness, and love that God gives you and help Him renew this world each and everyday. Spring is the season of new life. May your Springtime last forever.

May we always live by our true heritage. May we always Contribute our love, joy, and help to other human souls.

OUR TRUE HERITAGE

It seems as if Spring has finally arrived here in the mountains of my home. Today my heart and soul were filled full to overflowing with the countless blessings that come along with Springtime here. There was the glorious singing of the birds this morning that greeted both the new day and my soul with its joy. There was the beautifully enchanting song of the frogs this evening as I walked with my boys around the lake near my home. There was the spectacular sparkling of the sun off the lake water that seemed like a thousand angels dancing in delight. There was the tranquil peace of seeing a family of ducks making their home on the water.

The two most special blessings of this day, however, were the sight of smiling volunteers cleaning up the trash along the highway and the sight of the first flowers of Spring blooming along the walkway around the lake. What made these blessings so special was that they came not only from God, but from human hearts as well. Those flowers had been planted years ago by a loving soul to greet the people who came to the lake, and today's caring volunteers had made a special effort to remove some ugliness and bring some beauty back to the road that ran by its side. It was so glorious seeing these wonderful souls doing so much to help God bring a little more light and joy to this world. They touched my own soul with their work and their love.

Thomas Kinkade, the painter of light, once said that "Human souls are the only things in this life that continue forever. And therefore my true heritage must be my loving contribution to other human souls." May we always live by our true heritage then. May we always contribute our love, joy, and help to other human souls. May we always help God to make this world a better, more beautiful, and more loving place for all the beautiful souls in it.

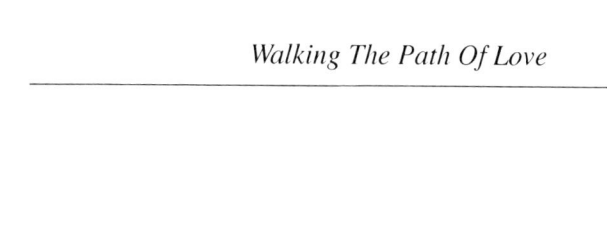

Each of us is reborn many times in our lives.

REBIRTH

Spring in the mountains of my home is a thing of beauty to behold. Clear skies and a golden sun make everything glow. Warm temperatures and gentle rains make everything grow. Tulips and dandelions each pop their heads out of the ground side by side. The trees are full of apple and cherry blossoms and their sweet fragrance fills the air. Butterflies emerge and begin to float happily from flower to flower. The morning air is full of the sweet songs of hundreds of birds. Bunny rabbits and deer sneak into the meadows before dawn to munch on the fresh, sweet grass. The gentle music of young children playing outside fills the ears with the sound of joy. Neighbors sweep off their porches and sit in their swings to take in the wonder all around them. It is a special time when the whole world seems to come back to life again.

Watching the rebirth of the Earth again this Spring has made me think of all the times in my own life when I felt dead inside only to be reborn. There have been moments of pain, purposelessness, and pride when I felt all the zest for life draining out of me. There have been times of despair, depression, and desperation when I never thought I would feel alive again. Yet, each time God in His love and wisdom has planted a few seeds in my soul that sprouted, grew, and gave life to me once again.

In truth, each of us is reborn many times in our lives. Each time we awake in the morning, we are reborn. Each time we rise up after we stumble and fall, we are reborn. Each time we invite our Creator into our hearts, souls, and lives, we are reborn. Each time we choose to love God, ourselves, and others, we are reborn. Each time we do a single, kind act, we are reborn. When it comes to rebirth the most glorious Spring still can't compare to us. May you make everyday of your life then a day of rebirth. And may you always live from the Springtime of your soul.

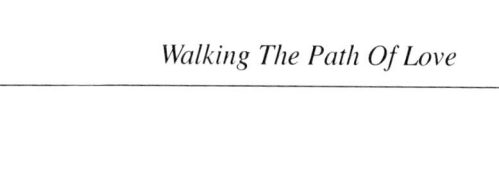

There is nothing sadder than passing by a treasure everyday and not seeing it.

APPRECIATION

Spring is continuing to work her wonders in the mountains this year. The skies are full of sunshine with only a few clouds floating on the wisps of the winds. My flower box is full to overflowing with purple phlox. A patch of bluebonnets sits proudly next to my front porch. A million dandelions dot the fields. Thousands of bees and butterflies are doing their best to help them flourish and grow. In the morning the birds sing their own "Ode to Joy" while in the evening a blanket of stars keeps you warm in the cool night air.

It seems too that this year I am appreciating Spring's beauty more than ever before. I am standing outside a bit longer in the morning to admire the rising sun and am staying out a few more minutes each night to gaze at the smiling moon. I am lying down on the warm grass to smell the flowers and am taking the time to rescue the few, stray moths that fly into my house. I am taking deeper breaths of the fresh, Spring air and am saying some extra "Thank You's" to God for giving us such a blessed time of the year.

Perhaps this greater appreciation comes from the long and difficult Winter we had this year or perhaps as I am getting older and wiser I am finally beginning to see the glory and majesty that was around me all the time. Either way I am grateful and happy. There is nothing sadder than passing by a treasure everyday and not seeing it.

This world is full of beauty, wonder, and delight. It is full of countless blessings given to us by our loving Father above. All we have to do is open our eyes to see them and open our hearts to feel them. Don't ignore these glorious gifts from God. Don't allow yourself to pass them by. Open the door of your soul and welcome them in. Let them warm you, nourish you, and strengthen you. Let them become one with you. Then go out and share their joys with everyone.

You have enough sunlight in your soul to ride out any storm life throws at you.

CRAZY WEATHER

We have been having some crazy weather here in the mountains of my home this summer. The other day, for instance, started out beautifully with a sunrise that could make the heavens' sing. The air was warm and the breezes gently kissed your cheek as you walked outside. The shining sun filtered through the leaves and lit up the world in a thousand different places. Just being outside lit up my own soul as well and I thanked God for another great day to be alive.

By afternoon, however, the weather had turned hot and muggy. The skies had become partly cloudy and the distant roar of thunder was in the air. As I went to run an errand it started to rain. Driving down the road I could still see the sun behind me but thick, grey clouds lay ahead. After only a few miles a gentle sprinkling of rain became a torrent that rolled down the roads and turned every pothole into a puddle. I stopped to go into a store but was drenched before I got three feet. Lightening flashes could be seen over the hills and I wondered if the storm would ever end. As I drove back home, though, the clouds parted and the sunshine reappeared. I arrived home soaked but safe and looked up to see the most glorious rainbow bridging the sky. I stopped in my dripping clothes to take in the sight and store it safely in the memories of my soul.

Life too can give us some crazy weather at times. Clear days can suddenly turn stormy in an instant. Sunny skies and gentle breezes can give way to pounding rains and lightening for no reason. Problems, troubles, and frustrations can soak you to the skin and you can find yourself wondering if the storm will ever end. When this happens take heart in knowing that God loves you through every type of weather and that you have enough sunlight in your soul to ride out any storm that life throws at you. Let that rain help you to grow and remember that the storms always end, the clouds always part, and sometimes you even get blessed with a rainbow.

May you always make your life as beautiful as a field full of dandelions.

DANDELIONS

The dandelions are back here in the fields around my home. My favorite flowers are always among the first to show up in Spring and among the last to leave in Fall. Their sweet, gentle beauty always warms my heart, delights my eye, and brings joy to my soul. They literally fill the lawns and meadows at this time of the year and continue on throughout the summer in spite of the countless attacks from lawn mowers and weed killers that they must endure.

I have loved dandelions ever since I was a little boy. I can remember picking handfuls of them to give to my Mom and seeing her beautiful smile when she smelled their sweet fragrance. I can remember too gathering hundreds of their blossoms so that my Grandma could make her famous dandelion wine. I can also remember using all the air in my lungs to help flower after flower scatter its seeds to the winds. I can remember most of all, however, just lying in the grass surrounded by these tiny, golden suns and wishing that summer would never end.

As I look out my window right now I can literally see thousands of these miraculous, little wonders sharing their beauty with the world. They remind me a lot of our own acts of love and joy. They are small but strong. They are sweet but hardy. They are simple but long lasting. They may seem tiny and insignificant by themselves, but if you fill a field or a life with them then Earth looks a lot more like Heaven.

May your days always bloom with loving acts then. May your mind always blossom with joyous thoughts. May your heart always flower with compassionate feelings. May you always feel the love of God sprouting up within you and around you. And may you always make all your life as beautiful as a field full of dandelions.

God wants us all to light up the Earth with our love and make it a bit more like Heaven.

A THOUSAND FIREFLIES

I was treated to the most delightful surprise the other evening as I walked out onto my back porch. As I looked out I saw what seemed like a thousand fireflies flying around and lighting up my backyard. It was such a joy watching each of them flash their light only to be answered in turn by dozens of others. It made me feel so connected to this world to see such a glorious sight. It made me feel so at one with God's love to be a witness to so much beauty. I stood out on my back porch for a long time just absorbing the wonder of it all and I gave thanks to God for letting me see it up close.

I have read that fireflies use their lights to communicate with each other. It seemed that this night, though, they were communicating with me as well. I saw their beauty and light not only with my eyes but with my heart and soul as well. My heart and soul filled with love and I smiled as one flew right by my face before lighting up its own body. It seemed to be telling me that I too could share a lot of light and love if I wished.

Maybe we all can take a lesson from our firefly friends. Maybe we all can begin to shine the light and love that lies within us. If we did I am sure that we would get the same results as they do. By shining our light and love brightly we would soon attract the light and love of countless others. Then together we would help to light up the world as well. Maybe this is why God gave us fireflies to gaze upon and enjoy. Maybe God wants to remind us to shine our own light, to share our own love, and to brighten the world with our joy. Maybe like the thousand fireflies in my backyard God wants us all to light up the Earth with our love and make it a bit more like Heaven.

One day we all will work together to help the fireflies chase the darkness away forever.

SUMMER LIGHT SHOW

It is going to feel like Christmas in July in the field behind my home for the next few weeks. My backyard buddies, the fireflies have finally returned to put on another Summer light show every evening for all of us to enjoy. It is such a delight seeing their little, golden lights blinking on and off just like the lights on a Christmas tree. It brings me such joy watching my whole backyard and the woods around it twinkle like it is Christmastime while the warm, summer breezes tickle my face. It reminds me that anytime of the year can feel like Christmas if you have love in your heart and light in your soul.

Still, there are times I feel a bit sorry for my firefly friends. They shine for only a brief time each Summer and their lights while beautiful last only a moment before fading again. In fact, I sometimes feel like a firefly myself. I try my best to shine long and bright with love, joy, and oneness with God, but it seems at times the most I can do is flicker. I am working hard, though, to leave my light on a bit longer each time and trying my best to make my moments of darkness less and less. I am asking God to help me everyday too and hope to one day shine more like a star and less like a blinker.

I hope that you are doing your best as well to shine bright and leave your light on in this life. I pray too that if you can't keep your light on all the time then you are at least blinking as much light, love, joy, kindness, goodness, peace, happiness, helpfulness, laughter, and caring as you can. Perhaps one day all of us will shine together and with God's help will create a summer light show that never ends. Perhaps we will not just help make everyday feel more like Christmas, but make everyday be Christmas. Perhaps one day we all will work together to help the fireflies chase the darkness away forever.

God loves you and meant for you to fly.

FLY

I have always taken the greatest joy in watching birds in flight. There is something so majestic, miraculous, and Heavenly in seeing them soar so effortlessly through the air. It seems that they are so very close to God as they fly above this world with such grace, beauty, and joy. I think they often remind us of how high our hearts and souls can fly too when we live the way we were meant to. Perhaps that is why artists throughout the centuries have so often pictured angels with wings.

The most amazing thing about watching these wonderful birds take to the Heavens, however, is the ease with which they do it. If you have ever watched a bird in flight then you will know that there is very little flapping of wings involved. The birds may flap for a little bit but then they catch a breeze and are soon gliding on the wind. They circle up and down and soar joyously through the air. It seems to take so little effort for them to fly and once they are flying they seem to stay in the Heavens forever.

I think that is perhaps why I love watching the birds so much. They show me that I too can soar through the skies with a heart full of love and a soul full of joy. They show me that I too can reach the Heavens when I share that love and joy with the world. They show me that I too can fly in my life with so little effort. Just by a few kind, loving, and giving choices each day I can catch God's breeze of endless joy and oneness and stay in the Heavens forever.

Don't stay grounded in misery then. God loves you and meant for you to fly. Let your heart and soul take wing and never look back. Let God's breeze of love and joy carry you to the Heavens. Let your life soar in delight and inspire others to take flight as well.

May you walk through life's fallen leaves knowing that the journey leads not to death but to eternal life.

AUTUMN OF OUR LIVES

    I love Autumn here in the mountains of West Virginia. The cool air and the hum of the heater in the morning soon gives way to the warm breezes flowing through the window fans in the afternoon. The delightful smell of dry leaves fills the air and in the evening I can sometimes catch glimpses of the deer feeding on the fallen apples from the apple tree in our backyard. The sound of happy children riding their bikes makes a sweet music for the ears as they play away the evening hours until darkness arrives. All of this wonderful joy takes place too under the brilliance of the mountains themselves. This time of the year they look like they were painted by Heaven's hand. Bit by bit the leaves on the trees transform into glorious golds, radiant reds, and outrageous oranges. Beautiful burgundies and browns soon appear too, as well as yellows that shine like the sun itself. This time of the year always gives me a hint of what Paradise itself must be like.

    It really amazes me then that the phrase "the Autumn of our lives" is always said with such fear. The very mention of it stirs up images of aging, illness, and approaching death. I guess so many are afraid of that last leaf falling that they fail to see the beautiful Spring that awaits them.

    I think the Autumn of your life should instead be embraced with joy. It should be the peak of a beautiful, colorful, and well-lived life. It should be full of choosing love, sharing happiness, and helping others. It should be filled with making yourself a better person and the world a better place. It should be overflowing with peace, understanding, and oneness with God.

    May the Autumn of your life then shine as brightly as the leaves on these mountains. May you live simply, love deeply, and grow daily. May your last days be your best days. And may you walk through the fallen leaves knowing that the journey leads not to death but to eternal life.

Our love and joy sometimes grow warmest when life is at its coldest.

BAD WEATHER AND GOOD HEARTS

It is amazing how even the worst times can be used by our loving God to bring out the best in us. I saw ample evidence of this recently when a fast moving Winter storm dumped an incredible two and a half feet of snow here. Cars were buried, businesses and schools were closed, roads were impassable, people were stranded, and tree limbs were snapped taking down power lines with them. A state of emergency was declared and it looked like the bad weather had beaten us all down. In the mist of all this misery, though, the best in everyone emerged.

We slowly came out of our houses, grabbed our snow shovels, and went to work. We started by shoveling out our drives and cars. We greeted neighbors doing the same. Then we started helping each other whenever we could. Snow blowers were shared. Paths were dug out so little dogs could have a place to walk and relieve themselves. Anyone with an extra snow plow attached it to their truck and cleared side drives while the state workers cleared the main roads. People who still had electricity thanked God for it and then went out to help those who had lost theirs. Electric line workers were tireless in their efforts to restore as many homes power as quickly as possible and every person whose home was lit back up smiled with a new appreciation for the energy they once took for granted. Families gathered around stoves, hugged each other in blankets, and looked out on the majestic mountains covered in snow. Then when the warm sun returned after days of cold they greeted it like a long lost friend. They watched the beautiful sunrise too like it was for the very first time.

All of this gave me a new respect for all the tough times and bad weather I have faced in my own life. I see now that God is always with us in our Winter nights as well as our Summer days. I see too that our love and joy sometimes grow warmest when life is at its coldest.

We are the ones, after all, who bring magic to the world.

ANGEL SLIDES

I was driving home today when I was blessed with a beautiful gift from the sky. It had been a wonderful sunny day with only a few clouds here and there. As I was driving home, however, I noticed that the light had dimmed a little. I glanced up to see a glorious sight. The sun had drifted behind a particularly huge billowy cloud. I could see the edges of the cloud glowing with light while wide shining sunbeams shot from it in all directions. My children and I call these sunbeams angel slides, because if you look closely enough at them you can see angels zooming up and down in the dazzling brilliance of them. They are one of the most beautiful things that you can see in this world and I always thank God when I gaze upon them.

I have often tried to share the magical sight of angel slides with others. Some people have been filled with joy and delight when they looked at them. Others have merely glanced up, shook their heads, and said they have more important things to do. I myself wonder what could be more important than the magic and beauty of life and the wonder of God's creation. We are all beings of magic, after all. We are all spirits of love and joy. We are all children of God dwelling in the oneness of life. What could be more important than realizing that and celebrating it?

The next time that you get a chance to experience the magic and beauty of life then grab it. The next time you get a chance to share joy, love, and the wonder of God's creation do so. We are the ones, after all, who bring magic to the world. We are the ones who bring Santa Claus, unicorns, elves, fairies, and angel slides to life in our hearts. We are the ones whom God's love flows through to bless the world.

There are few things better than watching a brilliant and beautiful sunset except perhaps watching a brilliant and beautiful life.

SUNSETS

If you can't remember the last time you watched the sunset then please watch the one tonight. If it is overcast then watch the one tomorrow night. There are few things that connect you quicker to God's love and joy than watching the sun setting over the mountains, or the ocean, or the desert, or the prairies, or the city. Every sunset is different and yet each one is so beautiful. Each one is full of fantastic colors from radiant reds, to glorious greens, to peaceful purples, to outstanding oranges, to breathtaking yellows. Each one is a masterpiece created by God's loving hand. Each one is a testament to His love for this world and for all of us.

There are few things better than watching a brilliant and beautiful sunset except perhaps watching a brilliant and beautiful life. Just like a fantastic sunset, a life lived from the soul is a thing of constant beauty. Its love and joy light up the sky. Its giving and sharing brings color and delight to the world. Its wonderful energy touches the hearts and souls of everyone around it. Like a glorious sunset, it too is constantly changing and becoming. It is never the same from one instant to the next, but is always growing towards greater joy, love, and oneness with God.

May we all live a brilliant and beautiful life then. May we all live from our souls and shine like the sun. May we all light up the sky with our goodness, love, joy, and delight. May we all use the clouds in our lives to bring ourselves to even greater beauty and wonder. May we all make our lives a fantastic sunset of goodness, kindness, energy, vitality, cheerfulness, merriment, and oneness with God. God loves us enough to give us a lifetime of spectacular sunsets. May we all love God enough to give Him a lifetime of glorious days lived in love, shared in joy, and celebrated in light.

Most of us are prodigal children at some point in our lives.

THE PRODIGAL CAT

My prodigal cat has returned! I found her meowing pitifully on my back porch yesterday after a week of living on the wild side. I was pretty sure that sooner or later the cold, November weather here would make her come home. Right now she is sitting on my lap while I type this, skinnier but wiser, gently rubbing her head on my arm and purring joyfully.

We first rescued our prodigal cat, Honey several years ago when she jumped into our open car without being invited. It appears Honey was on the run from several bigger and meaner cats at the time and was happy to find a pair of protective arms to rest in. The tiny calico soon made herself right at home too. Adjusting to an indoor life didn't seem to bother her at all. She was always first cat in the house to the bowl at feeding time and she loved to nap all day on the nearest available lap. She nuzzled and purred with the best of them too and was loved by all of us. This last year, however, Honey's wilder nature seemed to be calling to her. Several times she snuck outside on us only to return back after realizing just how tough life is out there. I am hoping that this latest outdoor romp is her last and that she finally realizes that struggling to survive in the wild just can't compare to napping on her Dad's lap.

My cat, however, isn't the only one who has made this mistake. I think most of us are prodigal children at some point in our lives. Just as in Jesus' Parable we wander away from our Heavenly Father and waste our days on wild living and foolish pursuits. Soon we find ourselves miserable, alone, and just struggling to survive. We return home to our Father broken, repentant, and hungry for His love again. Thankfully, God is always ready to forgive us and welcome us back into His loving arms once more. There is no better or more joyous place to be either, because it is the one place were we truly belong.

It is good to be loved, but it is even better to love.

IT'S GOOD TO BE LOVED

We have a saying in our house that goes, "It's good to be loved." It was inspired years ago by the wonderful love that our dogs show us everyday. I find myself thinking it first thing in the morning when the alarm goes off and I find a huge Saint Bernard head resting on the side of my bed waiting for its jowls to be scratched. I find myself saying it when my littlest dog whose belly is only a few inches off the ground still manages to jump up on my chair, climb up my chest, and lick my chin a hundred times. I find myself whispering it when my oldest dog who would be past eighty if he were human slowly gets up and walks across the room just so he can be petted and curl up at my feet. I find myself laughing about it when I see my daughter's young dog perched on the back of the couch like a squirrel watching out the window and waiting for her to get home. I find myself smiling about it when I go to feed my big, watch dog only to find him ignoring the food and cuddling up to my legs instead. I find myself thanking God for that love every chance I can and taking joy in that love every single day.

Each and everyday these five dogs show me just how good it is to be loved. Each and everyday these five dogs show me just how great it is to love. I am sure too that God put dogs here on this world to teach us just that. If everyone on this world were to love each other as unconditionally as our dogs love us then Earth would seem a whole lot more like Heaven.

It is good to be loved, but it is even better to love. My furry angels sent from God show me this every single day. May we all one day learn to love as freely, faithfully, and unconditionally as they do. May we all one day learn the lessons in joy, sweetness, playfulness, and happiness that they teach. May we all one day learn to live our lives as well as our dogs live theirs.

It is natural to be joyous, it is easy to be loving, and life is always wonderful when you choose to do both every single day.

AN OLD FRIEND

I am looking at an old friend of mine as I write this. He has been one of my best friends for almost twelve years now. He has blessed my life with his loyalty, kindness, wisdom, and love since the day that I first met him. It doesn't matter to me then that he has four legs instead of two, fur instead of clothes, and barks at me instead of talking to me.

As I watch my friend sleeping in the sun, I can't help but think of all the goodness he has brought into my life. He has been a protector of my children, a companion to all of my family and a fountain of love and affection to everyone he meets. He has been with me everyday through good times and bad. He has always reminded me that I am loved and showed me how to love at the same time. He has been more than just a little, 20 pound mutt that my father-in-law gave me. He has been rather a teacher, a friend, an angel in disguise, and a gift from God in my life and in my family's lives.

My friend has aged far quicker than me and has had more and more health problems over the years. I can see now the end approaching of his time with me. I am not sure how much longer we will have together before he passes from this world to await me in the next. One thing I do know, however, is that I will always thank God for bringing a tiny, mixed breed puppy into my life. This wonderful dog has showed me that it is natural to be joyous, that it is so easy to be loving, and that life is always wonderful when you choose to do both every single day. He has showed me again and again that you don't have to be perfect to be loved and that you can be happy in spite of all the difficulties life throws at you. He has showed me that poor health and old age might affect the body, but they don't have to diminish the spirit. He has shown me what it means to be a good friend and I will always cherish every single day we will have together.

A dog's love is unconditional. It reminds us of what God's love for us must be like. It shows us what our own love is capable of becoming.

A DOG'S LOVE

It was raining on the day I took my St. Bernard, Buddy to the vet for the last time. It was raining on my windshield, it was raining in my eyes, and it was raining in my soul. My heart was heavy with the sadness of knowing that I would soon be losing a friend who had always touched my soul with his sad face and sweet personality. When he was a puppy I used to carry him around in one arm. Now his 170 lb body was ancient and ailing. Throughout all his life he had protected us with his strength and loved us with his gentleness. He was a part of our family and taking him on this last ride was one of the hardest things I ever had to do.

My voice like my spirit felt broken as I told the vet that it was best to end Buddy's suffering now. I had watched over the last year as he slowed down. He was in a lot of pain. He seemed more and more irritable and uncomfortable with each passing day. Finally there came a point when I knew it was time to let him go. His days here on Earth may have been short by our standards, but every single one of them was full of love.

A person who didn't own dogs once asked me why I would put myself through such pain. Why would I bring dogs into my home knowing that eight, ten, or fifteen years later I would be losing them to death? I couldn't answer him at the time, but looking back on Buddy's years with us I think I can now. A dog's love is unconditional. It is pure. It is strong. It is blessed. It gives us such great happiness. It reminds us of what God's love for us must be like. It shows us what our own love is capable of becoming. A dog's love makes us better. If I have to suffer this pain then to have that love then I will do so gladly.

Take care dear Buddy until I see you again. You made me better. You helped me to love. You gave me so much joy. I will forever cherish in my heart the years we had here together.

Never pass up an opportunity to choose love.

CHOOSING TO LOVE

I know a young girl that gives so much love, joy, and light to this world. It doesn't matter that she has been confined to a wheelchair for most of her life. It doesn't matter that Cerebral Palsy has stiffened her muscles and made it hard for her to talk. It doesn't matter that she has to be helped with most of the physical tasks the rest of us take for granted. All that matters is that she freely gives love to everyone she meets. Her smile shares her joy directly with your heart and her eyes shine their light directly into your soul. The world is such a better place just because she is in it. She is a wonderful teacher to everyone around her of how to choose to love.

This wonderful young girl knows what is truly essential about life. She knows that it is choosing to love that gives life meaning, purpose, and happiness. She knows that giving love to others is the greatest gift we can give and that sharing joy with others is what we are here for. I think God must be smiling down on her when He sees all the goodness, love, and light her soul showers on this world.

I think of this beautiful young girl every time I find it hard to choose to love in my own life. Her glorious example reminds me always of how wondrous, fantastic, and delightful choosing to love can be. It reminds me of what God put us here for: to love, help, and care for each other.

Never pass up an opportunity to choose to love then. When you pass your child in the hallway give them a hug. When your dog or cat walks past your leg pet them. When you see a flower your wife might like get it for her. When you see a friend give them your smile, time, and kindness. When someone you care about is ill send them a card, a gift, and your prayers. Whenever you see someone in need help them. Always remember God put us here to love and choosing to love is choosing to live.

Is it possible to mourn someone you've never even met? Is it possible to cry for someone you have never even seen? Yes it is.

CONNIE

Is it possible to mourn someone you've never even met? Is it possible to cry for someone you have never even seen? My friend Connie passed away recently. She was just 68 years old. I had never met her face to face or even seen her picture. I had never heard her voice on the phone. I had never had the chance to give her a hug. She and her husband Charlie lived several states away from me and we never were able to visit each other like we had hoped to one day.

Connie and Charlie ran a newsletter about angel stories online and wrote me an e-mail once asking to use one of my articles. I agreed and with most people that would have been the end of it. Connie, however, had a joyous, youthful, laughing, loving, and playful spirit that found its way into everything from her marriage, to her friendships, to her work, and even to her letters. She and Charlie then quickly became my online friends. Soon they were sharing my writings with their readers every month. With each thing I wrote and shared I would get a letter of encouragement from Connie and Charlie. They were a gift sent by God above and I cherished their friendship. They touched my heart, uplifted my spirits, lightened my soul, and helped me to be a better person with just their simple e-mails.

When their e-mail address stopped working a few weeks ago I feared that their old computer had crashed. Sadly, it was something far worse. Connie has now passed into paradise, but the pain and loss lingers on for Charlie and all of us who knew her. Her love, her joy, and her light will outlast the pain, though. It will live on in all of us who knew her, forever.

Is it possible to mourn someone you've never even met? Is it possible to cry for someone you have never even seen? Yes it is. God bless you, Connie. Thank you so much for blessing all of us with your life.

Always look at life with the clear vision of your heart's eyes.

THE EYES THAT SEE

I have a blind friend who lives in New York City. Although we have never met face to face, we still write each other frequently. She is a remarkable lady and has become like a sister to me. Her optimistic and enthusiastic letters always lift my spirits and the inspiring poems she shares with the world always bring a smile to my face. She is all the more amazing due to the fact that she lost her sight halfway through her life. She had to give up her career and relearn to do everything that most of us take for granted. Many would have given up after such a loss but not her. Instead she embarked on a glorious new life full of award winning volunteer work. Her days are full of teaching English to new immigrants, counseling hurting hearts, writing, serving her religious community, and helping others in every way she can.

The light of my friend's example is a beacon that I try to follow as well. Whenever I feel too challenged in my own life I look at the challenges that she has overcome in hers. She may have lost her sight but she never lost her soul. She knows that the eyes that really see are the eyes of the heart, and she does her best everyday to follow the loving vision that they give to her. I am sure too that the eyes of the angels watching over her are always filled with tears of joy and that their faces are always full of shining smiles.

I hope then that when you go through your own life you are not distracted by the murky view that this world so often gives you. I hope that you see it for the illusion it is and instead look at life with the clear vision of your heart's eyes. God wants us to see this world and our lives through the eyes of love. It is only then that our sight will be pure. It is only then that our path will shine brightly before us. It is only then that we will see how we were meant to live and how we can best bring Heaven to Earth.

We all can become miracle workers if we choose.

MIRACLE WORKERS

This world is full of miracles from the rising of the sun at dawn, to the first flower in the Spring, to the colors of the leaves in the Fall. The miracles that touch my heart the most, though, are the tiny ones. These are the ones that go unnoticed by most people, but they are the ones that make life worth living.

One of the best of these tiny miracles is preformed by a local miracle worker everyday. Her job in this world is ringing up and bagging groceries, but her job from Heaven is bringing a little more joy to each heart she meets. I saw her hard at work just today. It had been a rainy morning with cold air and gray skies. Everyone who walked into the grocery store had a shiver in their walk and a frown on their face. I was no exception to this either. It had been a long, hard Winter and I felt tired as I bought extra bread and bananas to get me through the next coming storm. As I got to the check out line, however, the miracle worker went to work. She greeted me with a warmth that went straight to my heart. Her kind smile caused one to appear on my own face as well. Her shining, compassionate eyes reminded me once again that this is God's world and that it is full of loving souls like her. We chatted briefly as I paid for my food. As I left she told me to enjoy the day and I promised that I would. As I was walking out the store she was already uplifting the spirit of the next person in line. It occurred to me too that in all the years I had shopped there I had never once seen someone leave her counter without a smile on their face.

I thank God for that miracle worker and all the miracle workers of this world. The truth is we all can become miracle workers if we choose. We all can lend our strength, talents, hearts, and souls to making this world a better place. We all can bring a little Heaven down to Earth with our joy, laughter, and smiles. And we all can share the miracle of God's love every single day.

It is the insides that are essential. It is the insides that are eternal.

IMPROVING YOUR INSIDES

I was amazed recently when I read about how many different types of surgeries and treatments people are undergoing these days in order to look younger or more beautiful. There were breast and chin implants. There were injections to give you fuller lips. There were face lifts to take the furrows out of your forehead. There were botox treatments to take away your smile and laugh lines. There were liposuction treatments to take the fat out of your body. There were surgeries to make your nose smaller and tummy tighter. There were hair implants to take away baldness and dyes to take away any grey hairs that show up. There were skin treatments to take away age marks and liver spots. Some of these treatments cost very little, but others ran into thousands of dollars. It is strange what people are willing to do to look good on the outside.

When I look in the mirror lately at my thirty seven year old body, I see the wrinkles and laugh lines on my face, the greying and thinning hair on my head, and the little extra fat around my body. It doesn't bother me though. I feel more young and vital today than I did when I was twenty. I feel more alive and joyous now than when I was a teenager. I know too that I feel this way not because of what I look like on the outside but because of what I do on the inside.

It is the insides that are essential. It is the insides that are eternal. What you do everyday to improve your heart and soul will do more to make your life better than all the surgeries in the world. God made you a beautiful, loving soul that just happens to be carried around in a body. Keep your body healthy then, but keep your soul healthier. Take your plastic surgery fund and give it to charity. Watch a sunset. Give someone you love a hug. Do something good to help another soul. Live and love the way God meant for you to. Remember when you die only the love and joy within your soul goes with you. The rest really isn't that important.

The only thing that matters is the love within you and the love that you give to the world.

JOY IS FREE

I was driving down the road the other day listening to sweet music coming out of my car radio. My heart felt peaceful, my mind was clear, and my soul was full of love. Even with all its problems life seemed good. Then the music stopped and the news came on. There was talk of another millionaire celebrity in drug rehab after an incident with the police. There was news on the murder of a poor man whose life was supposed to be changed after winning the lottery. There was even a discussion on how much greed and excess had damaged our world.

Every story seemed to point once again to the old adage that money can't buy happiness. Hearing them made me think of a documentary I saw many years ago on Mother Teresa's home for the dying in Calcutta. What struck me the most when I watched it wasn't the grinding poverty there. It wasn't the sickness and suffering that the people there were going through. It was rather the peaceful smiles of love, kindness, and happiness that they shared with the Sisters and with each other. These people had nothing. Many were on the verge of death. Yet, they knew the simple truth that so many of us here are still learning: Joy is Free.

The truth is God loves you and wants you to be happy right now. He wants His light to brighten you, His peace to calm you, and His happiness to uplift you. He wants you to fill your life with His love and then share it with the world. He wants you to have joy and to spread joy everyday of your life here. Don't worship dollar signs and think that money will bring you happiness then. Joy can't be purchased. It can't be owned. It can only be chosen and then given freely to others. In the eyes of eternity money is only worthless paper. The only thing that matters is the love within you and the love that you give to the world. Make that your legacy and your life will forever be rich in joy.

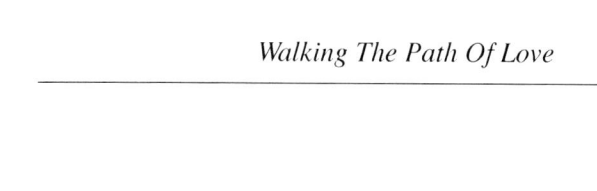

If you can't do what you love then love what you do.

WORK AND LOVE

My daughter was having trouble recently deciding on what to major in at college, so she asked my advice. I told her the one thing I wish that I had been told at her age: "Find a career that you love and you will never work a day." She caught me off guard, though, when she next asked what she should do if she couldn't get that career right away. What should she do if she had to take a job that she hated?

That question brought back a lot of memories of jobs that I had worked at over the years. I remembered one in particular. My young family was struggling. We had no money and there were no good jobs to be had in the area. My brother, however, was able to get me a job at a local lumber mill. The work was hard and meant constant pain for my back. Hours were spent loading and stacking lumber. The pay was just above minimum wage. In the winter the skin on my fingers split and bled from the cold, dry air. The job turnover was high. In the several years I worked there only the four of us supporting families didn't leave to look for something better.

Still, I also remembered singing hymns to myself while I stacked and loaded that lumber. I remembered the jokes and laughter we all shared during lunch and on breaks. I remembered as I pushed the lumber carts, glancing out the window and joyously watching the leaves changing in the Fall. I remembered how a simple sandwich tasted like the greatest gourmet meal in the world after 4 hours of hard work. I remembered thanking God for this job so I could feed my family. Remembering this gave me the answer I needed for my daughter. "Just bring your love to your job then sweetheart," I said. "If you can't do what you love then love what you do."

In this life we work to live, but we live to love. Without love work is drudgery. Yet, with love work is joy. May all of your working days then be full of love, joy, goodness, and God.

It is you who bring joy to your work.

THE HAPPIEST WORKER

I was in an office building the other day for an appointment. As I was sitting in the waiting room I watched several office workers hurry by. Their faces were full of seriousness and worry and not a single one had a smile. Each of them seemed full of stress and empty of joy. It saddened me to think that everyone of them had just started their work day and would spend another seven hours in this state.

It was then, however, that I noticed what had to be the happiest worker that I had ever seen. This person was actually singing while she worked. She had a smile for me, the others in the waiting room, and every other worker who passed her way. Several of those serious, worried, and unhappy workers that I had seen earlier, in fact, stopped to say hi to her. They soon were exchanging kind words and gentle jokes with her as well. It was clear that she was the real heart of this office building and not just the janitor who was mopping the floor.

This wise lady with a mop reminded me that it is not your work that makes you happy and it is not the world that makes you happy. It is rather you who bring joy to your work and you who make the world a happier place. God didn't create you to be miserable in this life. God brought you here to spread love and share joy no matter what your circumstances may be.

George Bernard Shaw once wrote that you should be "a force of nature instead of a feverish, selfish, little clod of ailments and grievances complaining that the world will not devote itself to making you happy." Let us all take his advice then. Let us all follow the beautiful example of a wonderful janitor I know and bring joy to our work, happiness to our world, and love to everyone around us. Let us all be joyous forces of nature and loving Children of God working to clean this world with our mops and to uplift this world with our smiles.

The real riches in this world can't be bought.

A WEALTHY WOMAN

I got to meet a wonderful person the other day. I had stopped to buy a local newspaper from a machine when I saw a middle-aged lady already there. She had a handful of quarters and was slowly buying paper after paper gently closing the machine after each purchase. She smiled at me and explained that her daughter's picture was in the paper. She was getting copies for all the members of her extended family.

When she turned to leave I noticed a hole in her shoe and realized that the rest of her clothes had also seen better days. She climbed into her rusty, 20 year old pick-up truck and after 30 seconds of trying finally got it started. She smiled at me again and waved as she drove off. It occurred to me as she disappeared in the distance that she had never once thought of taking the extra papers she needed while only paying for one. It was then that I realized I had just met one of the richest people in the world.

I only wish that everyone in this world had this lady's wisdom and wealth. She was rich beyond measure in all the important things in life. She was rich in honesty, integrity, goodness, kindness, cheerfulness, joy, and love. She was rich in family and in friends. She was rich most of all in oneness with God. It didn't matter if her truck was old, her clothes were worn, and her dollars were few. She was rich in her heart and soul, and she possessed within her the wealth of an entire Kingdom: the Kingdom of Heaven.

The next time you find yourself thinking and worrying about money then remember that the real riches in this world can't be bought. They must be chosen in your heart, created in your soul, and shared in your life. They are the love of God and the joy of living. And the more you give them away the more you receive them back in this life and in the next.

God doesn't want us to conquer the world outside of us. God wants us to enlighten the world inside of us.

STAND OUT OF YOUR LIGHT

There is a wonderful, old story about Alexander the Great that always helps to remind me of what is important in this life. Alexander after having conquered most of the known world and having reached the peaks of his power, fame, influence, and wealth was still left with a great feeling of emptiness inside of himself. Hoping to find some peace he decided to seek out a wise, old philosopher and ask his help. Alexander found the old man sunning himself on a hillside outside the city and approached him. Standing over the old man Alexander announced who he was. He then promised the old philosopher anything he desired in the entire world for his help. The wise, old man looked up at Alexander and smiling gently said: "only stand out of my light."

Perhaps all of us in this life who want peace, love, happiness, and joy should take a step back and stop standing in our own light. It is not, after all, what we have or what we achieve that brings us these things. It is rather who we are that brings them into our hearts, souls, and lives. If we want peace then we have to become peaceful. If we want love then we have to choose to be loving. If we want happiness and joy then we have to share our happiness and spread our joy.

All too often we seek to become like Alexander the Great and conquer the world outside of us. We seek fame, fortune, power, and prestige, yet even when we obtain them we find ourselves empty. God, however, doesn't want us to conquer the world outside of us. God wants us to enlighten the world inside of us. God wants us to fill ourselves with His love, joy, peace, and happiness. God wants us to be full of His light and then give it to the world through our laughter, our smiles, our words, our deeds, and our lives. May we all then make Heaven smile by praying, loving, and living so that noone not even ourselves can ever stand in the way of our light.

Nowadays money doesn't seem quite so important, but every loving hug I get from one of my children remains priceless.

GLUED GLASSES AND SEWED JACKETS

The longer I live the more I see that our souls' eyes and the world's eyes aren't the same. Just today, for instance, I was sitting at my kitchen table when suddenly my soul's memories took me back 13 years in an instant. I remembered sitting at that same table getting out a needle and thread to sew a rip in my jacket. It was one of many gotten from years of working in a lumber mill. That day, however, was my day off and I was enjoying every moment of it with my kids.

Suddenly my toddler climbed on my knee for a game of "blow on my belly". His giggles tickled my soul but his arm also accidently knocked off my glasses, breaking the frames for the hundredth time that year. At that time money was tight, miracle glue was cheap, and new glasses were not. I put my son down then, glued and reset the frames, and set them on the table to dry. Sewing the jacket without my glasses, though, was no easy task. On my thirtieth try at threading the needle my little daughter came in the room. I asked her if she could put the thread through the eye for me. She did on the first try and handed it back to me with a smile. "There you go, Daddy!", she said with sparkling eyes before heading back to her room to play.

I often wondered back then why I was having to struggle so hard just to get by. I wondered why I didn't have the money to buy the new clothes and glasses that others took for granted. Now thirteen years later I think that maybe God was having my soul spend that time learning what the true riches in life really are. That giggling toddler in my arms was one of them. That loving daughter with the sparkling eyes was another. Compared to them all the money in the world was just worthless paper. Nowadays money doesn't seem quite so important, but every loving hug I get from one of my children remains priceless. These lessons in love sometimes take a lifetime to learn, but what's a lifetime when seen from the eternal eyes of your soul.

My vast fortune is one of Love. It comes from knowing that when I love, I have joy.

THE RICHEST MAN IN THE WORLD

I was doing my monthly budget today. That is when you divide one check by ten bills and pray that there is a little something left over. The whole kitchen table was covered with bills, notebooks, stamps, envelops, labels, money orders, and my oversize calculator. I had just hit the wrong button on that calculator for the third time and was groaning with frustration when suddenly my little Beagle, Snoopy came racing out of my bedroom. Without breaking stride she bounced up on the chair next to mine and then leapt up on the table. She spun out on the papers sending them flying everywhere while my calculator crashed to the floor. Then without missing a beat she started licking my chin as fast as she could. I was about to yell at her but found myself laughing instead. Leave it to that sweet dog of mine to remind me that I am one of the richest men in the world.

My riches can't be placed in checking accounts or used to pay bills, but they are more priceless than a thousand treasure chests full of gold. My riches come from the furry friendship that follows me around on four legs all day long. My wealth flows from every smile that my children give me. My money comes in the form of hugged backs rather than greenbacks. My gems are the kind words and caring thoughts I give and receive. My gold comes from the shining spirits of my family, friends, and neighbors. My vast fortune is one of Love. It comes from knowing that God loves me. It comes from knowing that I can choose and share love myself everyday of my life. It comes from knowing that when I love, I have joy.

My bankbook may never be heavy, but when it comes to the treasures of Heaven my heart is full to overflowing. May you always choose God's love and Heaven's wealth yourselves. And may you always take the time to pet your dog even when she's sitting on top of your bills.

Walking The Path Of Love

Take whatever life gives you and use it to make this world a better, happier, and more loving place.

MY OLD CAR

Almost 20 years ago when I was still a college student I had an old car that I jokingly named Goliath because of its huge size. This car was older than I was at the time and drank more gas than a dozen pick-up trucks. It had rotted wiring that my dad had to replace more than once. The windshield wipers were broke. The battery died often. The radio didn't work and I only had one, scratchy cassette for the tape player. It often took quite a while to start and would backfire loud enough to be heard in the next county. My friends and teachers would often joke that they noticed buzzards circling my car when I was in class. Still, this was the car I depended on to commute long distances everyday and more often than not it got me there.

In a lot of ways too this car was a lot like life. The more you complained about it the worse it got. If I would complain about the gas milage one of the bald tires would blow out. If I would grouch about the sputtering engine it would start raining and I would be straining to see through the water all the way home. If I griped about not having a radio the next time the engine would not start at all. But, when I laughed about and accepted all of Goliath's problems it would run for weeks without giving me any trouble at all. I would pat its steering wheel with love and sing along to my old cassette tape as I drove home. God taught me a lot about life with that car.

My giant, old, beat-up car showed me that you have to appreciate what God gives you in this life. You have to rejoice in the good and grow stronger and more loving from the bad. You have to see that worrying and complaining only add to your misery and realize that you can select laughter, love and joy instead. You have to reach a point where you take whatever life gives you and use it to make this world a better, happier, and more loving place. You have to see that even if you start out driving a piece of junk in this life, God is still going to make it a glorious ride.

The more good fruits you plant and care for the less room there is for sour grapes in the garden of your life.

GOOD FRUITS OR SOUR GRAPES

I have noticed something recently. I am not as angry as I used to be. I am not as grouchy either. I don't complain nearly as much as I used to. I am not as worried or afraid as I once was. I can't think of anyone or anything that I really hate either. Now I don't think it is because I have mellowed with age. Quite frankly, I am not that old yet. Besides I know people a lot older than me who are a lot grouchier. I also know people a lot younger than me who are already way more mellow than I will ever be. Maybe it is that I just don't have as much room for those things inside me anymore. When life squeezes you what is on the inside comes out. If you are full of sour grapes then you will give the world vinegar. If you are full of good fruits then you will give the world orange juice. Maybe my good fruits are finally ripening while my sour grapes are dying on the vine. Maybe I am finally gardening my soul the way that God wants me to.

One thing I do know, however, is that the more you fill your heart, soul, and mind with love and thankfulness the less room there is for anything else. The more you love God, yourself, and others the less room there is for anger and hate. The more you thank God for your life and every good thing in it the less room there is for fear and worry. The more good fruits you plant and care for the less room there is for sour grapes in the garden of your life.

May you always fill your heart, soul, and mind with wonderful love and glorious gratitude then. May you always feel God's perfect love hugging your heart and uplifting your soul. May you always be so full of the good fruits of love, joy, and thankfulness that not a single sour grape can be squeezed out of you. Remember, you are the gardener and your life is the harvest. Plant well, water often, and always invite others to the feast.

May you spend the rest of your life making wrinkles from the glorious smiles and wonderful laughter you share.

MAKING WRINKLES

My daughter and I made a family scrap book for my dad's birthday this year. It was so much fun looking through all the old photo albums and seeing the pictures of my children, my mom, my dad, my grandma, my brothers, and myself through the years. It made me wonder what happened to those babies that I used to hold in my arms and to that hair that I used to have on my head. It made me wonder how many happy smiles and fun-filled laughs it took to make all those wrinkles I have on my face now. It made me wonder how our bodies can keep growing older while our joyful and loving souls never seem to age a day. Seeing all those pictures filled me with happy memories of loving times. It made me realize just how precious and wonderful our days here on Earth are and just how quickly they can go by. It helped me to see as well that life is a glorious journey that is best lived one delightful moment at a time.

I myself am looking forward to making the rest of my journey with a smile on my face, a song in my heart, and God in my soul. I myself am looking forward to a journey that is full of joy, laughter, and love. It doesn't matter if I make it with grey hair or with no hair. It doesn't matter if every smile and laugh I share on it causes my face to wrinkle a little more. It doesn't matter if my body keeps getting older on it, because I know that what is essential in us all never grows old and never dies.

May your own journey of life be a blessed one. May you rejoice in it moment by delightful moment. May you spend your days sharing your love, your years sharing your joy, and your eternity sharing your oneness with God. May you spend the rest of your life making wrinkles from the glorious smiles and wonderful laughter you share with everyone you meet.

It doesn't matter if you have 60 years, 40 years, 20 years, or 6 months left. You can still make it the best, most glorious, and most loving time of your life.

MY NEXT 40 YEARS

I was looking at the calender the other day and noticed that my 40th birthday is just a few months off now. I did a quick peek over each shoulder to see if that dreaded mid-life crisis was trying to sneak up on me. I didn't see a sight of him anywhere, and I doubt that he will show up at all. Yes, I have made more than my share of mistakes in my past that I am sorry for. My past, though, got me to where I am today. It made me who I am now. I can't change it. I can only learn from it and use it to better live the time I have left.

I am not sure how long I will have left on this world. None of us ever know when our time here will end. Some of us get a century and some of us get only a day. One thing I do know, however, is that if I get them: my next 40 years are going to be my best 40 years. I am going to love more, give more, and live more. I am going to sing more, laugh more, and dance more. I am going to smile more, hug more, and listen more. I am going to take in more sunsets, pet more dogs, and thank God more for my life. I am going to take more walks, watch more fireflies, and smell more flowers. I am going to choose more love, more joy, and more oneness with God all day long, everyday I am given. I am going to share it all with the whole world and show everyone everywhere that they can do the same. I am going to spend everyday I have left here bringing a little more Heaven to Earth before I leave Earth for Heaven.

It doesn't matter if you have 60 years, 40 years, 20 years, or 6 months left. You can still make it the best, most glorious, and most loving time of your life. The longest life here is still very short indeed. Do all you can then to live it in laughter, love, happiness, joy, goodness, and oneness with God. Then when you die and get to see God's smiling face you will know that your next billion years will be your best billion years.

My body may have the wear and tear of half a lifetime on it, but the soul that it is carrying around is as young as ever.

BIRTHDAYS

I celebrated my 40th birthday recently, and it wasn't nearly as scary as I thought it would be. In fact, it was a beautiful day full of laughter and happiness. The gifts, cards, and calls I received from everyone brought me so much joy. The birthday hugs and warm wishes gave me so much delight. The cake and ice cream made my stomach very happy and eating it with my loving family made my heart even happier. It was so wonderful feeling all that warmth, love, and caring. It made me thank God again for all the beautiful souls who have blessed my life.

I wasn't bothered by any of the getting old jokes either. I joined right in with them and laughed at the silliness of it all. I have never been afraid of being middle-aged or growing older. Having thinning hair just means there is less I have to comb in the morning. The grey ones tend to sparkle in the sunshine better as well. I have always loved my wrinkles too. They are the living proof of a million smiles. And while my body may have the wear and tear of half a lifetime on it, the soul that it is carrying around is as young as ever. It is ageless and eternal, and I am doing my best to always live from its wisdom, love, joy, and light.

None of us knows how many birthdays we are going to have left in this world. I think then that we should all make everyday here our birthday. We should rise with a smile on our face and a "Good morning God" on our lips. We should spend our days giving out hugs, spreading laughter, and enjoying all the wonderful things we have been blessed with in this world. We should spend our time sharing kind words, doing loving acts, and thinking joyous thoughts. We should stop rushing around, sit down, and enjoy some cake and ice cream with those we love. Then on our first birthday in the next life we can smile as the angels sing, "Happy Birthday" and look back on our time here with happy memories and a joyous soul.

I'm not nearly as old as I used to be.

AS OLD AS I USED TO BE

The grocery store is a great place to get food for your body, but I have found out recently that it can be an even better place to find food for your heart, soul, and mind. This happened the other day as I was walking through the local store to get some oatmeal. Two elderly ladies were standing by the fruit section catching up on old times. The first one jokingly asked her older friend how old she was now. The older lady answered loudly and to everyone's delight: "Honey, I'm not nearly as old as I used to be." Everyone within ear shot laughed when they heard this including me. I realized too as I was walking out of the grocery store that I am not nearly as old as I used to be either.

I am not nearly as old as I used to be when I constantly worried about my bills and how I was going to pay them. Now I just trust in God and I always seem to have more than enough. I am not nearly as old as I used to be when I fretted about my weight and my thinning and graying hair. Now I just look in the mirror and smile. The body may look a little older, but the soul on the inside is younger than ever. I am not nearly as old as I used to be when I was always judging others, being angry with them, or worrying about what they thought of me. Now I just do my best to judge noone, love everyone, and share my joy with the world. Life I have found is too short to live any other way.

You don't have to be as old as you used to be either. God made all of us both ageless and forever young. By choosing love, joy, and oneness with God you can always keep growing younger and younger on the inside. By sharing that love and joy you can give your youth, energy, and vitality to the world. By living from your soul you can stop counting your birthdays, start living for eternity, and always know that you will never again be as old as you used to be.

Whether you are a new clock, an old watch, or an ancient timepiece remember that you still have time to make a wonderful difference in this world.

MY OLD WATCH

    I have had the same watch now for twenty four years. It was a gift from an uncle that I got when I was just fourteen. It was one of the first digital watches ever made and it weighs about two pounds. I have gone through about five watchbands with it so far. Some of the numbers on the display are getting hard to read as well. Still, I keep buying new batteries for it and refuse to get a new one as long as this one works. My wrist feels strange without its familiar weight on it and my heart still feels a touch of warmth from my late uncle's love when I look at it.

    A part of me too is reassured when I look down at this old timepiece still working away after all these years. It gives me hope for myself in the years ahead of me. This body of mine just turned thirty eight years old recently which means that if I live an average life span on this world then half my life is already over. Since a large part of the first half of my life was spent figuring out what life is all about, this only leaves me the last half to really live my life the way it was meant to be lived: in choosing and sharing love, joy, and oneness with God. I take hope then in seeing my old watch still working away after most watches are thrown away. It reminds me that I can keep working away too and bring a little Heaven to Earth, no matter how old I get.

    Whether you are a new clock, an old watch, or an ancient timepiece remember that you still have time to make a wonderful difference in this world. You still have time to warm some hearts with your love, touch some souls with your joy, and heal a few lives with your light. You still have the time to live like you were meant to, to love like you were born to, and to be one with God like you were designed to be. You still have the time to bring a little Heaven down to Earth and to ready your soul to fly from Earth back to Heaven.

When it comes to eternity age is a number and the body is a liar.

GROWING YOUNG

As I have moved into my forties now I have begun to see more and more that body age has very little to do with soul age. My body keeps telling me again and again that I am getting older. My soul, however, seems to laugh at the thought. Just this morning I awoke to an aching back and stumbled into the bathroom. I stretched and popped my back as much as I could and then looked in the mirror. My thinning salt and pepper hair was mostly salt. My forehead was lined with deep wrinkles and my frowning face made me look like a tired, middle-aged man.

This depressed me but only for a few seconds. Then I remembered that whether I grow old or grow young is very much up to me. I said, "good morning" to God, thanked Him once again for my life and smiled in the mirror. Amazingly, the wrinkles in my forehead disappeared while the laugh lines around my eyes grinned with joy. My sleepy eyes began to sparkle and I watched as fifteen years disappeared from my face in a second.

No matter how old this body of mine may get my soul remains young. This is true for all of you as well. Whether you are 18, 48, or 80 you can still live with the love and laughter of an 8 year old. When it comes to eternity age is a number and the body is a liar. The only years that matter are the years you spend loving others.

Before you get lost looking for the fountain of youth then, take a look inside of yourself. You may find that your spirit is still young, vital, happy, and wrinkle free. You may see that the ability to give love and share joy knows no age. You may realize that when it comes to eternity our lives are here for only a brief moment in time. God created your soul and God created the body that carries it around. One is temporary, but one is forever. Don't spend too much time then worrying about the one that won't last when you can be living for the one that will.

The table of life is filled to overflowing with a fabulous feast of goodness. Yet, so many people gaze upon it and never take a bite.

EAT EAT

When I was a boy growing up we always had a huge Italian dinner every Sunday after Church. We would arrive home with the hymns still singing in our ears, the smiles still shining in our eyes, and the hundred hugs still tingling on our bodies. Soon our noses would join in the celebration as the wonderful sauces that had been cooked the night before began to simmer. The rich tomato sauces were full of meatballs, sausages, chicken, and potatoes. The spaghetti being cooked was always enough to feed an army. Everyone always ate their fill as stomachs, taste buds, and hearts all grew happier. Those meals were always occasions of great joy, love, and delight. It was a time of sharing, of abundance, and of family.

Life I think is often like those dinners. There are so many good things to eat. There are so many wonderful things to celebrate. There are so many glorious things to enjoy and to share. The table of life is filled to overflowing with a fabulous feast of goodness. Yet, so many people gaze upon it and never take a bite. It is so sad to see so many starving souls out there refusing to take a single nibble of the endless love, joy, peace, and happiness that is just sitting there waiting to be eaten.

Don't let the dinner of life pass you by. Don't sit there starving in your soul when joy, love, and light just wait for you to choose them. My father used to always say "Mangia Mangia" which is "eat eat" in Italian whenever we sat down to one of those fantastic dinners. That is my advise to you as well. God has prepared a wondrous feast of life for you. It is full of love, joy, peace, happiness, goodness, kindness, laughter, fun and delight just waiting to be chosen and just waiting to be shared. Pull your chair up to the table of life, invite everyone to join you, and Eat Eat.

It is those who never say they're sorry who end up living sorry lives.

ASKING FORGIVENESS

My Grandma whom we all called Nanny was a solid, first-generation, Italian immigrant. She came to this country with her family on a tiny ship during World War I when she was only 8 years old. During the trip she survived stormy seas, little food, and an attack by a German U-boat. After getting here her large family worked hard to build a new life in America. They never had much money but were rich in love. Nanny grew up, married, and raised 4 sons of her own. And then when my parents moved back into her home she helped to raise me too.

One day when I was about 5 or 6 years old my parents and brothers went on a trip. It was just me and Nanny in the house for the weekend. Nanny seemed so happy to be taking care of me all by herself. She made me a special breakfast that first morning. I was too young, selfish, and foolish to see that then, however. All I could do was complain about how the food was not how Mom always made it. Nanny quietly put down the plate and went into the living room. I followed a minute later and saw that she had tears in her eyes. It was the first time I had ever seen my strong, rugged, and proud Grandmother cry and I was the one who had caused it.

I walked over to Nanny, climbed on her lap, and for the first time in my short life I did something else too: I apologized without being told too and asked Nanny to forgive me. She smiled, rubbed my head, and told me I was a good boy even though I didn't feel like one then.

That memory just like my Nanny's love will stay in my heart forever. It is strange that so many people think it shows weakness to admit your mistakes and say you are sorry. In truth, it is a sign of both strength and wisdom. Asking forgiveness helps us to learn, to grow, and to love. It brings us closer to Heaven and blesses us with God's love. It helps us to become the people we were meant to be. It is those who never say they're sorry who end up living sorry lives.

We all need more adventures that excite our hearts and nourish our souls.

ADVENTURES

Growing up in my grandmother's house as a boy was always an adventure when the relatives would visit. The food would be filled with extra garlic, parsley, and other spices. The smell of homemade bread and slow cooked tomato sauce would fill our noses with bliss. The dinner later would fill our stomachs with spaghetti and meatballs and our hearts with contentment as well. The air would be filled with Italian words both good and not so good. The talk would be excited and you always knew to sit a few feet away from those talking so that a hand gesture or waving arm didn't accidently hit you in the face. There would be more laughter, more stories, and more jokes than you could keep track of. There would be more hugs, more tears, and also more smiles as well. It was always such a beautiful adventure in living. You could always feel the love and joy flowing from heart to heart and from soul to soul.

I wish the world had more adventures of this type. We all need more adventures that excite our hearts and nourish our souls. We all need more adventures in becoming the people that God meant for us to become. We all need more adventures in loving, laughing, giving, and caring. We all need to share more smiles together, more hugs together, and more tears together. We all need more family dinners. We all need more simple evenings filled with talk and togetherness. We all need to spend more time remembering how we are all one family put here by God to love each other and to share joy with each other.

I hope that all of your adventures are loving ones then. I hope that all of your adventures bring you closer to God. I hope that all of your adventures help you to share your heart's love and your soul's joy with your family, your friends, and the entire world.

Your Heavenly Father loves you joyously, powerfully, and perfectly. Have faith in His love.

FAITH

"What does faith feel like?" That was the question a friend sent me in a letter the other day. As I was thinking about how to answer him a single memory kept coming back into my mind. I was 5 years old and very sick. The doctors told my Mom that my tonsils were swollen, infected, and needed to come out. Surgery was scheduled for the next day and I spent the night in the hospital with my Mom sitting at my bedside. She told me gently not to be scared, that she was there for me and would be right here when I woke up after the operation.

The next morning the nurses gave me something to sleep before surgery and the last thing I remembered before going under was seeing my Mom's smiling face. That is until I suddenly woke up to find myself surrounded by strange adults wearing masks. I had come to just before the operation was to begin. My young heart was filled with terror and I sat straight up and screamed "Mommy!" as loud as my painful throat possibly could. The next thing I remembered was seeing my Mom's loving smile again in the recovery room. She held my hand, whispered words of comfort, and brought me a bowl of ice cream. Even though my throat still hurt I wasn't scared anymore. I felt loved and everything seemed right with the world again.

That is what faith feels like to me. It is feeling loved, cared for, and watched over. It is knowing that no matter how painful or scary life gets you need only to call out to God and He will be there for you. It is having the gentle touch of His hand on your spirit and the loving whisper of His voice in your heart. It is even enjoying the delicious, ice cream filled days of happiness that He gives you here. Most of all, though, it is knowing that you are His Child. Your Heavenly Father loves you joyously, powerfully, and perfectly. Have faith in His love then. Rejoice in your birthright. And share your love with the world.

Give the gift of a few loving thoughts yourself today. Why let the angels have all the fun?

A LOVING THOUGHT

George Macdonald wrote that "If instead of a gem or even a flower, we should cast the gift of a loving thought into the heart of a friend, that would be giving as the angels give." I can remember one of the first loving thoughts that was cast into my own heart and the angel who placed it there. I was a young boy and my parents, brothers, and I were spending the afternoon at the home of a family friend. This friend was the hymn leader at our church as well as the music teacher at my grade school. I remember I used to sit and listen to her play songs on her guitar for hours at a time. On this day my dad was outside once again working his mechanic magic or her ailing, old car. My mom was setting up a picnic for everyone and my brothers were in the yard playing. I was inside talking with our friend and listening to her sweet music. I don't remember exactly what we were talking about, but I do remember at one point her saying, "Joe, for someone so young you already understand a lot about life."

That loving thought made a home in my heart that day. Before it I never cared much about understanding life, but just as a seed grows into a flower those kind words by that caring angel awakened a desire in me to understand as much as I could about life and living. It helped me start a journey that is still going on today. That gem of an idea that I could really understand what life was all about and that I could live my life as it was meant to be lived shined in my soul and kept me searching, learning, and growing.

That loving thought led me through pain, sorrow, and back home to God again. It led me to writing, sharing, and who I am today. It led me to the knowledge that God is love, that life is joy, and that we are all here to love and help each other. I hope you cast the gift of a few loving thoughts yourself today then. Why let the angels have all the fun?

Do your best to tend your own garden. Sun it with your smiles, water it with your joy, and keep the weeds away with your kindness. Let its roots grow deep in oneness with God.

TENDING YOUR GARDEN

When I was a boy growing up we had four separate gardens growing around our house to help feed us through the year. We grew corn, green beans, squash, watermelons, cantaloups, onions, tomatoes, and carrots. The biggest garden of all was devoted entirely to potatoes. My Mom and Grandma also had countless flowers growing in boxes around the house and hanging in pots on the porch. It was wonderful to be around so much life and so much growth. It makes me admire even today the power, intelligence, and love of God to create so many wonderful, living things.

I, of course, grumbled like any little boy when it came time to plant, weed, and water so many gardens. I much preferred riding my bike. Still, seeing how much love, attention, and work my parents put into the gardens, seeing the cellar full of fresh canned vegetables for the winter, and seeing the wonderful foods that always showed up on our dinner table left lasting memories in my heart, soul, and mind. Even though I only have a few flowers in my own garden these days, I still water them with a smile and laugh when they stretch and grow towards the sun.

I also try to take special care of my other garden as well. That garden is my life. I do my best to keep it free of weeds, to nourish its roots in God's love, and to water it daily with my own joy. I do my best to grow the greatest fruits, the best vegetables, and the most beautiful flowers in it, because I want to share this glorious garden with the whole world.

Do your best to tend your own garden then. Sun it with your smiles, water it with your joy, and keep the weeds away with your kindness. Let its roots grow deep in oneness with God. Let its plants grow strong in beauty, happiness, forgiveness, energy, and delight. And then share all its goodness, bounty, and abundance with those around you.

The table you set will be a true feast grown in the Eden of your own loving soul and bathed in the light of Heaven.

The real riches of life come from every act of giving, helping, and sharing we do.

GIVING YOUR LIFE AWAY

Sometimes the greatest lessons in life come at the oddest moments. One of mine came when I was helping to harvest our gardens as a boy. We had four of them and they took a lot of work. In the fall, however, they produced more than enough vegetables for the whole year. Every year my Dad would separate a part of them to share with friends and people in the community. One time while we were loading up a bag full of corn to take to a needy family I asked my Dad why we always gave so many of our vegetables away. He said, "Son, not everyone has as much as we do. They can use our help. Besides, if we didn't give these vegetables away they would just go to waste." Now that I have been on this world a lot longer I can see the wisdom in my Dad's words. I can see too that they apply not just to vegetables but to our entire lives.

What good are our lives, after all, if we don't give them away? What good are the things we have if they just go to waste? We all come into this world naked and shivering with nothing. We can take nothing with us when we leave here either. Our lives and possessions then are only momentary gifts. They have meaning only when we share them and use them to help others.

In fact, the real riches of life come from every act of giving, helping, and sharing we do. These true riches are love, joy, and oneness with God. They are the wealth of the spirit and the treasures of Heaven. The best thing about them too is that they never run out. The more you give them away, the more God pours them into your heart, soul, and mind.

Don't let your life go to waste. Give it away. Give it joyously in service to others. Give it lovingly in service to God. Give your money, your time, your talents, your help, your skills, your energy, and your love. Give without fear knowing that God will always give you back even more. Make yourself rich in the treasures of Heaven and bring a little Heaven to Earth as well.

You can't live your life always looking in the rear-view mirror.

LOOKING IN THE REARVIEW MIRROR

When I was a young boy my family would always make a Summer trip out of state to visit my Grandma and Aunt. It was a long drive over curvy, mountainous roads. It often took up to eight hours to get there. This was before the age of i-pods and DVD players too. My Dad didn't care much for the rock music the radio stations played in the nineteen seventies either, so the trip was a quiet one. Stuffed in the back seat of the family sedan with my two brothers, I only had one thing that I could do and that was look out the window.

A window seat was best for scenery watching, but being the youngest and the smallest I was always stuck in the middle. That left gazing over my brothers' shoulders or looking through the rearview mirror at what we had just passed. The second option, however, could never be done for long. With mountain roads I never knew when the next curve was coming up and if what I was looking at didn't match what my body was feeling then I was carsick in minutes.

After a few times of my stomach turning flip flops I learned my lesson and kept my eyes on the road ahead. That way I could gaze in wonder at the golden light of the sun shining down on the green leafs of the trees as we drove by them. That way I could enjoy seeing the deer peacefully eating grass along the side of the road. That way I could delight in what was coming next instead of being sick over what was already left behind.

Those long trips taught me that you can't live your life always looking in the rearview mirror. If you want to enjoy the beautiful moments of today then you have to see them as they happen. God doesn't want us to live in the past. He wants us to embrace the joy that each new day brings. He wants us to realize the preciousness of every second and use them all to love Him, ourselves, and others. Keep your eyes on the road ahead then and trust God to lead you Home.

We are all one family in this world in need of both food and love.

WANT SOME CRACKERS?

When I was growing up every Summer my family would pile into our old car and make the 8 hour trip over the mountains to spend a week visiting my Grandma in Tennessee. Each year too my Grandma and Aunt Charlotte would make us an early Thanksgiving dinner. The table would be full of mashed potatoes, turkey, gravy, corn, yams, sweet potatoes, green beans, rolls, butter, pumpkin pie, and whipped cream. It was a feast of love and we would relish every bite of it.

During one of those visits on the day of our big meal, I met a new boy in the neighborhood while playing outside. His mom and he had just moved into town after his dad had left them. Like most young boys we became friends right away and spent the rest of the afternoon playing and talking. After we were pretty worn out from all of our adventures he invited me over to his home. It was older house that had seen better days. He said his mom was renting it and was away at work but that we could get a snack if we wanted. We searched the kitchen but there was nothing but empty shelves. I was shocked. I had never seen a house with no food in it before. Finally I heard, "Want some crackers?" My friend had found half a box of crackers and a peanut butter jar with a tiny bit left in it. He told me not to worry. His mom was getting paid soon and would fill the shelves again. Still, I didn't eat any of his crackers that afternoon.

That evening as I sat down to our early Thanksgiving dinner I looked at all the food and realized that my new friend had given me a gift. For the first time I was truly thankful to God for everything on my plate. For the first time too I truly saw the need in another's life.

I never saw my new friend after that. They moved again later that year. I still pray for him even today, though. He opened my heart that day to gratitude and compassion. He made me see that we are all one family in this world in need of both food and love.

Focus on what is essential, what is eternal, and what is truly important in this life: loving each other just as God loves us.

A FIRE IN THE NIGHT

I can still remember that late summer night when I was eleven. I can still remember my Grandmother's scream that woke me from my sleep. I can still remember my brother grabbing me out of bed and yelling that there was a fire in the house. I can still remember the confusion as we all ran through the smoke filled rooms towards the front door. I can still remember my Mom seeing our little dog at the last instant and picking him up as we ran out the door. I can still remember all of us standing there wearing only the night clothes we were sleeping in while my Grandma's 50 year old house burned to the ground in a matter of minutes along with everything we owned. The flames that burned down our house also burned that memory into my mind forever. I can still see my Mom, Dad, brothers, Grandma, and I standing there crying and wondering what we were going to do after losing everything we had.

It was only later that I realized that God in His love and goodness had, in fact, spared us from losing the one true treasure each of us had: our lives. Every essential thing that we needed had come out that door with us. Our hearts, minds, bodies, and souls were all unhurt and that was all we needed to live in love and joy again. We were still a family. We were still together. We could still hold each other, laugh, and share our love and happiness at being alive. Soon thanks to the goodness of our community and extended family we had replaced what material things we had lost and moved into another home. I would never again, however, consider the things of this world as important as the love we share from our hearts and the joy we spread from our souls.

One day all the things we now own will like that house turn to ashes and dust. Let us not waste our lives living for them. Let us instead focus on what is essential, what is eternal, and what is truly important in this life: loving each other just as God loves us.

We are here to love each other.

ONE THING

I can remember what a scary time it was after our home burned down when I was a boy. We weren't sure where we were going to live. We had lost everything in the fire. We didn't even have any clothes to wear. Thankfully, we were surrounded by caring people. Our church, community, and extended family all rushed to help us. It was such a blessing seeing this outpouring of love. I can remember too during this time the moment that I stopped being afraid. A woman was bringing some winter coats into the temporary home we were renting. When my Mom thanked her she said, "Honey, that is what we are all here for." I knew then that everything was going to be alright, because I realized that we are all here to love each other.

Sometimes it amazes me how often we forget this. Life is so simple and yet we make it so complicated. We rush around trying to do a million different things that we think are so important. In the end, though, there is only one thing that matters and that is Love. All of life comes down to this one thing. It is the one thing we are meant to learn. It is the one thing we are meant to do. It is the one thing we are meant to choose. And it is the one thing we are meant to share. It is what life is all about.

If you want to live then you need to love. You need to love God. You need to love yourself. And you need to love others. You need to bring some winter coats to a family in need. You need to cheer up a sick friend. You need to help a neighbor fix up their home. You need to hold a crying child in your arms and comfort them. You need to offer a word of encouragement and kindness to a hurting heart. You need to take the hand of a loved one and let them know just how much you care about them. You need to smile and give your joy to everyone you meet. You need to do the one thing that makes life worth living. It is, after all, what we are all here for.

Life sure is one crazy ride. Enjoy every minute of it.

CRAZY RIDE

I can remember once when I was a boy our family went to an amusement park while visiting my Grandma in Tennessee. My older brothers were riding all of the big rides and I really wanted to get on one as well. Finally my Mom agreed to get on a mini roller coaster with me. The ride operator started the ride out slow but soon we were going faster and faster while my Mom's face got whiter and whiter and she held my hand tighter and tighter. Finally the ride started to slow down and we thought it was just about over. Suddenly, however, we heard the operator's voice yell out, "Do you want to go backwards?" Sixty teenagers screamed out "YES!" and a half a second later I heard my Mom scream out "NO!!" as loud as all of them put together.

I can sympathize with how my Mom felt. A lot of times in this life I have wanted to stop this crazy ride and just get off. The roller coaster has just kept moving along, though, with twists and turns that made my heart flutter and my face turn white. I used to think that if I could just get everything right in my life then this ride would smooth out and I would be happy. Yet, everyday new problems, troubles, and frustrations would appear. There was no getting ahead of them, no getting around them, and no off switch on the ride.

I finally realized one day that this crazy, roller coaster ride was my life. There wasn't going to be any slowing down or smoothing out in the future. In fact, there was every chance that I would end up going backwards as well. The best that I could do then was to choose love, joy, and oneness with God while I rode it. The best that I could do was to laugh and enjoy the trip instead of screaming my head off. The best that I could do was to smile, take the frightened hands of those riding with me, and trust in God to see us through every twist and turn this ride might take. Life sure is one crazy ride. May all of you enjoy every minute of it.

Our greatest work here is in the hearts we touch, the good we do, and the love we share.

WORKING IN JOY

When I was a boy we had a wood stove that heated the house in the Winter. Keeping that stove full was no small task. My Dad, two brothers, and I would spend days cutting up trees on our land to fill the woodshed. It was hard work splitting up the logs, tossing them into the back of the pickup truck, and stacking them into cords. We never complained however. We spent the time laughing, joking, and teasing each other. We knew that hard work was a part of life and was best done in joy. We knew too that this hard work would keep us warm during the long, cold Winter to come.

Putting food on our tables and heat in our homes is only a small part of our real work in this world, though. Our greatest work here is the hearts we touch, the good we do, and the love we share. Our hands may be able to lift a log into a truck, but our smiles can lift another's heart in joy. Our arms may be able to carry a load of wood, but our kindness can help someone carrying a heavy load in their life. Our skills and talents may be able to make us some money, but our love, goodness, and oneness with God can help to make this world a better place forever.

Leo Buscaglia said, "To work in love is to work in joy, to live in love is to live in joy." Don't be afraid of a little hard work then. Do all of your work in love and in joy. Work at giving, work at loving, and work at living happily ever after, day by day and choice by choice. God put us here to grow, to learn, to work, and to love. God put us here to find joy in our efforts and to share love in our lives. Do all of your work with a smile on your face, with love in your heart, with joy in your mind, and with light in your soul. If you do so your work will become play, your life will become joy, and God will always work through you.

Walking The Path Of Love

Sometimes we forget that we were meant to fly and we need the children to remind us.

FLYING HIGH

I was driving down the road on a warm, Spring day recently with my windows rolled down. I wanted to feel the wind on my face and smell the wonderfully sweet scent of the flowers in the air. It was my ears, however, that were blessed with sweetness as I slowed down for a school zone. The laughter of dozens of children filled the air as they ran and played on the playground. I heard several of them yelling with delight as they swung on the swing set. With each pass they flew higher and higher. It brought a smile to my lips, a warmth to my heart, and a flood of memories to my mind.

I remembered being their age. Us boys would always give the girls a push and then jump in the empty swings next to them and try to catch up. With our legs pumping we would soon be soaring through the air. We laughed at the thrill of freedom, at the joy of flight, and at the feeling that at any moment we could zoom into the heavens. I remembered later being a young father and pushing my own children on the swings. Watching their happiness was a bit of Heaven itself. I remembered as well one time my five year old daughter saying, "You swing too, Daddy!" I was embarrassed at first but once I saw my feet headed towards the clouds again all those wonderful feelings of childhood came rushing back. I was flying high once more. After that I always swung with my kids no matter who was there to see me.

I think that sometimes we forget that we were meant to fly and we need the children to remind us. God didn't put us in this world to sit and suffer with our feet in a mud puddle and our eyes on the ground. He wants us to fly higher and higher in love, joy, and wonderful oneness with Him. He wants our spirits to soar into Heaven while still here on Earth. And most of all He wants us to give a push skyward to anyone who needs it. Love well and fly high always.

I never did outgrow my appreciation for my Father's forgiveness.

A FATHER'S FORGIVENESS

When I was a boy I always wanted to be a cowboy. I remember my Mom worrying about me getting sick from the heat in the summer, because I wore a thick blue sweater all the time. No respectable cowboy, however, would wear short sleeves so I sweated while I played.

I was overjoyed too when one day my parents gave me a bb gun. It looked just like a lever action rifle that all the cowboys used in the movies. I spent hours each day during those summer months shooting at stumps and pretending to be John Wayne. I even mastered the one-handed, swing, cock and shoot move I had seen him do in a movie once. At least that is what I thought. As I was coming into the house one afternoon, though, I tried it one time too many. The gun that I thought was empty let out a soft pop and a bb flew across the room and parted the hair of my Dad who was asleep on the couch. My Dad took one look at the bb hole a half inch above his head, walked over to me, took my gun, walked outside, and calmly broke it in half.

I didn't cry too much over this. I knew how close I had come to hurting my Dad with my stupidity. I didn't expect to ever get another bb gun either. That is why I was so surprised when my Dad bought me another one the next year. I guess he thought I had wised up enough to know how to use it this time. I never put a single bb in the new gun, but in my imagination John Wayne rode again.

I eventually outgrew my cowboy stage, but I never did outgrow my appreciation for my Father's forgiveness. He showed me that even when I messed up in the worse way I was still loved. He gave me another chance and let me know that I was forgiven whether I deserved it or not. He shared with me some of the unconditional love and forgiveness that our Father in Heaven has for us all. May we always embrace and share that love and forgiveness as well.

Let's stay connected to things far more important than the internet.

STAYING CONNECTED

When I was a boy there were bikes to ride but no cell phones to text on. There was a river for swimming but no world wide web for surfing. There were basketballs to bounce but few video games to play. There were paths to walk but no reality televison shows to watch. When we did sit in front of the tv we could choose between two channels and had to go outside and turn the antenna to get in the second one. When we wanted to make a call too we had to sit in the chair next to the phone, pick up the receiver gently to make sure noone else was taking on the party line, and then slowly dial each number on the rotary wheel.

These days my home is wireless and yet has more wires than I can count. I have a mobile phone, cell phone, and computer. I have two televisions and a hundred cable channels. I have CD and DVD players. My daughter has an i-pod and a cell phone with more functions than she could ever hope to use. I am connected with friends and family all over the globe and can communicate at the speed of light. I am a part of the vast electronic web encircling our world.

I know too that there is no going back to the simpler age that I grew up in. Still, there are times each day when I shut down my computer and turn off my televisions and cell phone. I do so to spend some quiet time in prayer, to talk to my children and hear about their day, to chat with my friends and neighbors, to read a good book, to pet my dogs, and to take a walk outside and watch the birds flying across the sky. I do so to stay connected to things far more important than the internet. I do so to stay connected to God, to love, to life, to humanity, and to my own soul. Without these connections technology is nothing more than a meaningless distraction.

Use your technology wisely then. Stay connected not distracted. Live your life, share your love, nourish your soul, and make this world a better place both online and off.

Every act of kindness we do touches another's heart. Every bit of goodness we share makes the world a better place.

THE LETTER

When I was a freshman in college I received a letter that forever opened a window in my soul. I had just started writing and the editor of my local county newspaper had been kind enough to publish some of my work. About a month later the letter arrived. Sadly, I lost it in the many moves I have made since then, but it's essence still lives in my heart.

Here is what it said. "You may not remember me. We last saw each other in kindergarten and my family moved the next year. We still get the county paper in the mail, though, and when I saw your name I had to write you. You see that first year in school was very difficult for me. I was a tiny, sickly, and homely girl that the other children teased everyday. The thing I remember about you is that you never did. You were always kind to me. When we lined up to go out the teacher always put me beside you and you would hold my hand as we crossed the street. You talked to me and played with me. When you were around too the other kids didn't tease me. You saw me as a person, not someone different and I will be forever grateful for that. My whole life was better because of how you treated me all those years ago."

I quickly wrote back to my kindergarten friend and we corresponded happily for several years before the illness that she had struggled with since childhood finally took her life. I will never forget, however, just how much that simple kindness I had shared meant to her. It made me see that kindness, goodness, love, and joy truly are the most important things in the world.

Every act of kindness we do touches another's heart. Every bit of goodness we share makes the world a better place. Every choice for love we make brings us and those around us closer to God. God blessed us with the power to help, heal, love, and change this world forever. Let's use that power and make both Earth and Heaven smile.

My Mom and Grandma may have left this world, but in my heart and soul my arms will always surround them.

TWO ARMS NO WAITING

I got to hug my Mom and my Grandma again today. It felt so good that for a moment my heart leapt for joy and my eyes filled with tears. In that second the whole world was full of love and the Earth felt like Heaven. Then it was over, because I awoke from my daydream.

You see, my Mom and my Grandma both died years ago. I enjoyed every hug we shared over the years they were alive, but now I see I didn't hug them nearly enough. I don't know why I kept my arms and my heart closed so many times over the years. I don't know why it took me so long to realize that you can't take love or life for granted. If I had it to do over I would have hugged them a dozen times a day, every single day they were with me. If I could have those moments back I would have followed the example of my own son who gives me more hugs everyday than I can count. I would have taken the lead of my son's childhood friend too. She may be confined to a wheelchair but she can still hug your heart out with the squeeze of her hand or lift your spirits with a smile that is brighter than the noonday sun. If I could live those years again I would do so with my arms, my heart, and my soul wide open.

Thankfully, God in His love gives us a lifetime to learn from our mistakes. I can't live those years again, but I can live today. I can love today. I can share a hug today. My Mom and Grandma may have left this world, but in my heart and soul my arms will always surround them.

I hope that you share a few hugs yourself today. I hope that you hang a sign on your heart that says, "two arms, no waiting." I hope that you give your love to all those around you. I hope that you shine a smile to everyone you meet. I hope that you fill your every phone call, letter, or e-mail with "heart hugs" as well. Life is short. Time flies. Our days here are brief. Don't pass up a single chance then to love, to share, to help, and to hug.

I realized a while ago that I had spent far too much of my own life looking out a window waiting for something or someone to bring me what I wanted.

A TAP ON THE SHOULDER

A long time ago when my full grown children were still "children" I saw something that still brings a burst of joy to my heart whenever I think about it. My youngest son who was still a toddler at the time was very attached to his big sister. When she first started going to school he would stand by the window waiting everyday for her bus to bring her home. And when I would walk her up the hill to our house he would be waiting at the door to hug her.

One day, however, after a particularly nasty diaper incident his Mom needed to give him a quick bath right when the bus was scheduled to arrive. When his sister and I made it to the door then he was still in the tub. His sister went into her room to put her coat up and as soon as she shut the door out toddled her brother from the bathroom and right to the window he went. His internal clock knew that his sister should be home any second. I smiled as I watched him looking intently out the window while his sister emerged from her room. Quietly she snuck up behind him and ever so gently tapped him on the shoulder. The look on his face when he turned around and saw his big sis was one I have rarely seen in this life. It was pure bliss, pure joy, and pure love. His big eyes shined with delight, his toothless smile took up most of his face, and his tiny arms opened up to give his sister a very big hug.

I realized a while ago that I had spent far too much of my own life looking out a window waiting for something or someone to bring me what I wanted in this life. It took me a long time to finally feel the gentle tapping on my own shoulder. When I turned around there was God ready to take me in His arms and fill me with His love. I saw then that everything I had ever needed: love, joy, peace, and oneness with God had been with me all along. I had just been looking the wrong way. I hope that you too will turn around when you feel that tap.

We are all Children of God full of the magic of love and the miracle of joy.

BOX OF BOOKS

In my bedroom beside my bed there is a box full of magic, miracles, wonder, delight, love, joy, and imagination. It is a box of books that I used to read to my children when they were young. Through the years I have read hundreds of different books to them, but the ones in this box always remained their favorites. In it are fairy tales, Christmas stories, and myths of wisdom handed down through the ages. In it are books full of humor, intelligence, acceptance, giving, helping, growing, and learning. In it are wonderful stories designed to teach children how to live wisely, kindly, lovingly, and joyously.

I hope that my children learned a lot from those books. I know that I learned a lot from them myself. I learned that life is full of miracles, full of wonder, full of beauty, and full of magic when we live it with love and joy. I learned that no matter what challenges we may face we can overcome them with a happy heart, a caring mind, and a soul full of oneness with God. I learned that God loves us more than we will ever know and that love shines most brightly in the eyes of little children. I learned as Hans Christian Anderson said that "Every man's life is a fairy tale, written by God's fingers."

That old box of books remains by my bed even though my children are too old to be read to anymore. It awaits my grandchildren or any child I am called to babysit or to care for. It waits to share its wonderful stories of magic and miracles, light and delight, wonder and wisdom, love and joy, and goodness and God. It waits to touch another child's heart, brighten another child's mind, and warm another child's soul. It waits to remind this adult once again that we are all Children of God full of the magic of love and the miracle of joy.

No matter how much we may wish it life doesn't come with a rewind or a pause button and can only be lived moment by moment.

PAUSE FOR A MOMENT

Do you ever wish that life came with a pause button? Do you ever wish that you could just take a moment from your life and stay there forever? I was remembering a moment like that from my own life recently. It was the night I brought my newborn, baby son home from the hospital. My son was 3 weeks late in arriving and my wife needed an emergency Caesarian section to bring him into the world. She was still in a lot of pain and sleeping when I heard him wake up during the night. Gently I picked him up and carried him into the living room so my wife could sleep. Rocking him in my arms I told him how much I loved him and how I would always be there for him no matter what. Then I saw his sweet eyes gazing up at me and the smallest of smiles form on his lips. It was a moment of pure joy that I wished would never end.

Over the next 21 years I watched my son grow into a wonderful young man. In spite of having to deal with Autism he has still spread more joy, shared more love, and shined more light than I could ever hope to. He has brightened up every room he has ever walked into and he has filled my life with so many happy moments. My only regret is that I let far too many of them go by without cherishing them as I should have.

Still, no matter how much we may wish it life doesn't come with a rewind or a pause button and can only be lived moment by moment. Do your best then to embrace each moment as it comes. Celebrate each and everyone of them as a gift from God. Cherish the moments of love you give and the moments of joy you share. Learn from your moments of pain and grow from your moments of failure. Most of all, though, take the time to pause for a moment right now and give thanks to God for your life and all the moments of happiness it has brought you. Life may be momentary but the love it gives you lasts forever.

We are all souls in bodies sent here to choose love, to share love, and to learn about love.

MY SONS

Raising two sons with Autism has been the most difficult challenge that I have ever faced in this life. Watching them deal daily with their handicaps and trying to help them in every way I can has at times been painful, frustrating, and even heart-breaking. Through it all, though, I have gained more wisdom about living than I could have ever imagined. My two sons have been my teachers as well as my students on how to live and how to love. They have taught me more than I could ever have learned on my own and they continue to show me more each day.

I have learned from them that I am no better than anyone else in this world. I may be able to do some things that they can't, but their lives are just as precious and just as valuable as mine. As I watch my oldest son be a friend to everyone in his school and share his simple kindness with everyone he meets I am warmed to the depths of my being. I know too that he has touched hearts and brightened souls everyday of his life here with his gentle spirit and smiling face.

I have learned too from them that we are all Children of God. We were all created by the same loving hand. We are all souls in bodies sent here to choose love, to share love, and to learn about love. When I look into my youngest son's shining eyes I can see that loving soul within. He may not be able to say more than a few words, but his laughter, smiles, and hugs speak volumes. He may face a lifetime of challenges, but he will still be teaching the world about love and joy everyday of it.

Having these two sons has shown me just how much God loves us and just how much God wants us to love each other. I try then to share my love and my joy everyday with them, with my beautiful daughter, with my loving family, with my wonderful friends, and with all of you special souls who read my simple words. I hope that you all do the same.

The simpliest life can do limitless good in the eyes of Heaven.

A SHINING SOUL

My youngest son is severely handicapped by Autism. His speech is limited. He cannot relate well to other people. Learning is difficult for him. The smallest problems can seem like the end of the world to him emotionally. Tiny changes frustrate and upset him greatly. His life is limited in many ways. Still, when he hugs me, looks me in the eyes, and smiles I can see his soul shining through. His soul that I see twinkling in his eyes and glowing in his smile is full of love, joy, goodness, and God. Even though it is trapped in a challenged mind, it still is beautiful, powerful, and limitless. Even though it lives in a life far different than mine, it still spreads its love, joy, and light to this world.

I am doing my best to follow the example that I see in my youngest son's shining soul. I am doing my best to share my own love and joy in spite of my problems and limitations. I am doing all that I can to bring goodness, peace, happiness, and delight to everyone I meet. I am doing all that I can to let God live through me and to make this world a better and more loving place for all of the people out there no matter what their problems and limitations may be.

No one has to live a limited life. No matter what limits your body, mind, or situation may have you can always let your soul shine through. The simplest life can do limitless good in the eyes of Heaven. A hug, a wave, a smile, a kind word, or any tiny act of love is priceless in the eyes of God. Every life here no matter how small touches countless others with its love, joy, and light. Remember then as you travel the pathway to Heaven to scatter a little soul shine along the way. The sun may light up the Earth, but a shining soul full of God's love lights up the Universe.

The next time you see a person trapped in a handicapped body or mind don't look away, look within. If you do you will see a brother or sister who wants and needs your love.

SEEING THROUGH AUTISM'S WALLS

I pulled an old photo album from its shelf yesterday and wiped the dust off of it. It is one that I rarely open, but something moved me to open it then. Inside of it were baby pictures of my youngest son from the day of his birth until he was 18 months old. Looking at them made my heart ache, not with nostalgia but with loss. You see, the reason I hardly ever look at these pictures is that I can see in them the normal child my son could of been. When I look at those happy, intelligent, and shining eyes in the photos I can see all the years of learning, growing, and becoming that my son could have had before the autism came.

The severe autism that came upon my son in his second year stole his language, changed his personality, and forever clouded his mind. It left him with a life of frustration, mood swings, compulsive behavior, and mental pain. Each day now is a struggle for him and although I try to make his life easier and give him as much love and joy as I can, in the end the autism is always there keeping him from being the person he could have been.

One thing, however, that brings me joy is that everyday I can see his gentle spirit break through those autistic walls around him. Sometimes it is in a laugh, sometimes it is in a smile, sometimes it is in a hug, but it always lets me know that a loving soul still lives within him. One day in the life after this one I hope to get to talk to that sweet spirit and thank him for all the love he gave me and all that he taught me about patience, compassion, and life.

I am going to try and look at those old pictures more often now. I want them to remind me of who my son truly is: a Child of God, a Being of Light, and a Spirit full of Love. The next time then that you see a person trapped in a handicapped body or mind don't look away, look within. If you do you will see a brother or sister who wants and needs your love.

My children truly have taught me far more than I have taught them.

MY CHILDREN

I am continuously amazed at how I raised such wonderful children. The latest example came when my family and I were swimming at a local pool. A lovely, young woman came up and introduced herself to me and my wife. She was a graduating valedictorian from our local high school and just wanted to tell us how much she had enjoyed the kindness and friendship our oldest son had shown her in his first year of high school. He was her friend and a friend to so many others in spite of the struggle of having to deal daily with the handicap of autism. His goodness and kindness left an impression in her heart and her words made me thank God again for blessing me with a son like him. He truly is a Child of God and an angel in disguise.

My oldest son, however, isn't the only angel that I have been blessed to raise. My daughter continues to delight me with her strength, love, maturity, joy, and sweet soul. At a time when most teenage girls are taking it easy over the summer, she is volunteering at the summer reading program and helping to instill a love of learning and a joy of living in the hearts and minds of younger children. My youngest son too continues to bless others everyday with his life. Although his autism is even more severe than his brother's he still lights up the hearts and souls of those he meets everyday with his sparkling eyes, beautiful smile, and infectious laugh.

My children truly have taught me far more than I have taught them. They have shown me again and again how the true measure of living is how much love you give and joy you share. They have shown me again and again what God wants us all to know: that we are here to help each other, care for each other, and spread delight into each other's lives. They have shown me again and again that when you love unconditionally, give goodness freely, and share joy without expecting anything in return that God blesses your life in countless, miraculous ways.

When it comes to choosing and sharing love and joy the teachers often become the students and the students often become the teachers.

YOUNG TEACHERS

I was taking my youngest son to grade school the other day when I saw one of my daughter's former teachers. We talked for a moment and she shared how much she missed having my daughter in class. She said she rarely had a student so kind, helpful, and willing to learn. This wonderful teacher's kind words made me smile, and I thanked her when she gave some of the credit to me. I knew in my heart, though, that as much as I have taught my daughter how to love and how to live in this life, she has taught me even more.

It is funny how after all these years I find that I am still learning how to live and how to love. It is even funnier too that so many of my teachers are younger than I am. I think that when it comes to choosing and sharing love and joy the teachers often become the students and the students often become the teachers. I am so happy that I got three of the best in my kids. My youngest son's Autism keeps him from saying much but he can still teach a lot when it comes to love and joy. His smile and laugh light up every room he enters and his happiness always brightens everyone else's day. My oldest boy too still struggles with Autism, yet his caring and kindly spirit have made him more friends in his young life than I will ever have in mine. He has a Master's Degree when it comes to Kindness and a PhD when it comes to Love.

I am so thankful for my young teachers and so blessed that God sent them here to be my children. Even while I continue to write about and share love and joy in my own life, I know I will always be a student of these things as well. It is why we are all here, after all. We are here to learn how to love, to teach others how to love, and to share God's love everyday of our lives. The classroom on love is always open in this life and in the next. Don't overlook your own young teachers then. You may learn more from them than you ever dreamed possible.

Every bit of love that we give plants another sapling of Heaven here on Earth.

CHANGE THE WORLD

My daughter and I planted four trees in our backyard recently. They were little more than twigs when she brought them home. She was able to hold all four of them in the palm of one hand. Still, with faith in the future I dug the holes in our backyard and with loving care my daughter planted each one of the saplings. When I look out on them now I smile. They are so small and yet so full of life. As they stretch towards the morning sun and slowly grow upward to the sky I can see the hundreds of glorious years that lie ahead of them. Soon they will be filling the air around them with life giving oxygen. Soon they will be blessing the world with their sweet smell and comforting shade. Soon they will be changing the world for the better just by being in it.

What most of us don't realize is that we can change the world for the better just by being in it too. When we go out of our homes each morning we don't see just how many trees of goodness that we can plant each day. Every single smile that we share plants a little more light in another's heart. Every single act of kindness that we do plants a little more kindness and happiness in this world. Every single moment of joy that we spread puts new seedlings of joy in the souls around us. Every single bit of love that we give plants another sapling of Heaven here on Earth. We may only think of ourselves as tiny twigs, but in our lifetimes we all can do more good than a forest of Redwoods.

Don't be afraid to try and change the world for the better then. Remember that you are a Child of God put here to fill this world with love and joy. With God's love in your heart and with God's joy in your soul you can help to create a never-ending forest of goodness in this world just by planting one sapling at a time.

Walking The Path Of Love

With God's loving hand steadying your walk you can use your other hand to reach out and help up those who have fallen as well.

HOLDING HANDS

My sons and I decided to go walking around the lake near our home the other day. It is such a glorious place to spend an afternoon in the Springtime when the leaves are coming out on the trees and the flowers are coming up through the ground. It has a well worn gravel path that circles the entire lake. You can walk at your own pace and delight in all the natural beauty that surrounds you. It is the perfect place to get back in touch with God and to fill your soul with joy.

The only problem is that with the path being so near the water, erosion sometimes causes holes to develop along the walkway. It was while we were walking along it the other day that one of these holes caught my oldest boy unawares. He stumbled and almost fell but thankfully was able to reach out and take my hand. I steadied him and we walked on for awhile holding hands and feeling connected in our love for each other.

I think that sometimes the troubles we face in our journey through life are a lot like those holes in the ground. They are always there causing us to stumble and sometimes even to fall. It is good to know, however, that we can always reach out and take the hand of our Heavenly Father. He is always there by our side waiting to pick us up and steady us. He is always ready for us to take His hand and walk on with Him connected in love forever.

The next time you stumble and fall on your journey through life then reach out and take God's loving hand. And after you take it never let it go again. Walk on with God forever, choosing love and sharing joy with each step you take. Always remember too that with God's loving hand steadying your walk you can use your other hand to reach out and help up those who have fallen as well. The journey through life, after all, is always better when you are holding the hands of those you love.

I want you to make a promise that you will never only half-live another day of your life.

NOW

I got a letter and picture from my sponsor child today. It was so amazing to see how healthy, happy, and beautiful she looked. It made me feel so good inside to know that just for a bit of money each month I am able to make her life so much better.

The thing, however, that amazed me the most about her picture and letter was just how much she has grown up over the years. She has become a wonderful young lady who is full of grace, maturity, and love. She has become so very wise, kind, caring, and giving. She has gone from a happy child to a joyous girl on the verge of becoming a woman.

Seeing her letter reminded me once again of how fast children grow up and how fast life flies by on this world. Seeing her letter reminded me once again of how precious every second we are given is and how we should never waste any of them. I have heard so many people say how they would love to do so many wonderful things in their lives, yet they never do them. They put them off and put them off. They go by day after day only half-living and only half-loving.

I want you to make a promise today then. I want you to make a promise that you will never only half-live another day of your life. I want you to make a promise that you will choose joy now, choose love now, and share them both now. Now is the only moment you can live. Today is the only day that you really have. Yesterdays are only memories and tomorrow is only a dream. You must live today. You must live now. Do you want to tell someone you love them? Do it now. Do you want to pray to God and feel His love and joy within you? Do it now. Do you want to sponsor a child overseas, give you own children a hug, and share your goodness and talents with the world? Do it now, do it now, and do it now. God loves you so very much and He wants you to live in love and to live in joy right now.

I could never be a Scrooge myself, because I have the Spirit of Christmas Love and Joy sleeping down the hall from me.

THROUGH HIS EYES

My oldest son is always the first to get the Christmas Spirit in our house. He usually gets it a few weeks before Thanksgiving. It is a joy to watch. With both the heart of a child and the soul of an angel he cherishes everything about this time of the year. He takes so much happiness in putting our decorations up. He takes so much pleasure in our evening drives to look at the outdoor lights on other people's houses. He takes so much delight in singing in the school choir's Christmas show. He laughs and smiles though every Christmas movie we watch. He enjoys all the Christmas music in the air. He always shakes the hands of the Salvation Army bell ringers while I put cash in their kettles. He always enjoys the presents we get him too, but the present he gives us is far more precious. That present is seeing the way he lives with so much peace and happiness every single day of his life. He is the embodiment of the Christmas Spirit all year long.

I am sure that God and all the angels must be smiling down as they watch this "special" son of mine. He lives the way we all should live. He sees the beauty of the world, the miracle of life, and the love of God in all things. He awakens the Christmas Spirit in me and everyone else he meets. I could never be a Scrooge myself, because I have the Spirit of Christmas Love and Joy sleeping down the hall from me. I only wish that the whole world could see Christmas and life through his eyes.

My simple Christmas hope then is that all of you try to see life with the same joy, love, kindness, peace, happiness, wonder, and delight that my son does. If you do this you truly will be giving yourself a glorious gift. If you do this God and His angels will always be smiling down on you. If you do this everyday will be Christmas.

The gifts that most touched my soul are the ones that came from the hearts of those around me.

THE BEST GIFT

The stores are going to be crowded the next few weeks. It is that time of the year between Thanksgiving and Christmas when people go shopping for special gifts for those they love. As I started to think back on the gifts I have been given over the years, however, it wasn't the ones that came wrapped up under a tree that moved me the most. The gifts that most touched my soul are the ones that came from the hearts of those around me.

Those special hugs my Grandma gave me as a boy that squeezed the air out of my lungs and warmed my heart at the same time are a gift I will always cherish. The gift of my Mom's loving and joyous smile still lives on in my heart and soul today. I always felt happier when I saw it. Those boyhood touch football games my brothers and I had in the sunshine, rain, and even the snow are a gift of fun that still makes me laugh. The countless repairs my Dad made on my tired, old cars over the years is a gift I can never repay. His help kept me driving and his love kept me going during some of the toughest points in my life. Those phone calls from my Aunt that keep me smiling for half the day are another priceless gift I still enjoy. They always lift my spirits as high as Heaven. The hugs, smiles, laughter and kind words that are shared with my children, my friends and my neighbors are daily gifts that I wouldn't trade for all the presents in the world. The letters and cards I get from my wonderful online friends also have a special place under the Christmas tree in my heart. They have made my soul rich beyond compare.

All of these gifts remind me too that Love is the greatest gift of all The love that God has for us and the love that we share with each other is what life is all about. Love gives meaning to our days, joy to our hearts, and wealth to our souls. It makes us brighter, the world better, and brings

God closer. May you always have the time of your life then giving the best gift of all.

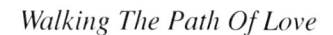

The true meaning of Christmas doesn't come from lights, decorations, or presents.

THE WORLD'S UGLIEST CHRISTMAS TREE

I can remember when I was a young boy how we always used to go into the woods around our home to cut down our Christmas tree. There always seemed to be the perfect pine just waiting for us to cut down and decorate with happy hearts. One year, though, when I was no more than five years old I was allowed to go on the tree hunt. As we hiked through the woods I saw probably the ugliest, most lopsided, and scraggly pine tree ever. To my five year old heart, however, it seemed like a great choice. I can remember my Dad cutting it down over my brothers' protests and my Mom decorating the weak, sagging limbs as best she could. I still have an old picture of me and my brother standing in front of the world's ugliest Christmas tree.

What warms my heart about this memory is that my Mom and Dad didn't mind if the tree didn't look good or decorate up nicely. They only cared that I loved it and wanted it for our tree. They knew that the true meaning of Christmas didn't come from the lights, decorations, or presents. They knew the true meaning of Christmas came from the love and joy we shared with each other and the love that God had for each and everyone of us.

These days my tree is artificial and I smile when I look in the woods and think of all the ugly, little Christmas trees I am saving by having it. The love and joy I share with my family and everyone else remains the same, though, at Christmas time and all through the year. It is a glorious gift from God that keeps on giving and giving and giving. It is like John Greenleaf Whittier once wrote: "Somehow not only for Christmas but all the long year through, the joy that you give others is the joy that comes back to you." Merry Christmas to you. May your tree always be full of light and your heart always be full of love.

If there is one gift I could give to each of you at Christmastime and every day of the year, it would be the knowledge that you are loved.

YOU ARE LOVED

One of the warmest Christmas memories that I have was the year that I was Santa Claus. I was a young, substitute teacher with a new family just starting out in life. I was called in to work at the local grade school on the last day before the Christmas holidays. Near the end of the day I was summoned to the principal's office and asked to be the Santa who visited all the classrooms. Being a great lover of both children and Christmas I agreed.

I can still remember going from classroom to classroom doing my best to sound both old and jolly at the same time. I was about 50 pounds heavier then so I had the round little belly part down fine. My beard, however, was another matter as it kept sliding halfway down my face. I think that more than a few of the kids recognized me, but it didn't matter. They still rejoiced in seeing Santa. They still laughed and delighted in their small gifts and candy canes. They still felt joyous and happy. They still knew that they were loved and that was all that mattered.

If there is one thing that I could give to each of you at Christmastime and every day of the year, it would be that knowledge that you are loved. You are loved and watched over by a greater love than you could ever imagine. You are loved by God who made you, who delights in you, and who wants you to be happy. In all the difficulties, problems, and heartaches this world brings, you are loved. In all the obstacles you must overcome, challenges you must face, and pain you must go through, you are loved. In all the mistakes you make, times you stumble, and wrong paths you take, you are loved. You are loved every second of everyday of your life with a glorious love that will never end.

Know that you are loved. Know that God loves you always. Rejoice in this love with the joyous heart of a child. And then like a jolly, laughing Santa go out and share it with the world.

Christmas truly is about Love. It is about loving each other just as much as God loves us.

A GIFT OF LOVE

I have always loved Nativity scenes ever since I was a boy. I remember growing up seeing the great care my Grandma always took unwrapping ours. She would gently lift each ceramic statue out of the box and lovingly arrange them in the tiny, wooden barn. The baby Jesus was always the last one lifted out and she would always smile before placing Him in the manger.

It was at another manger too that I saw the most beautiful picture of the real meaning of Christmas. This was years ago when public Nativity scenes were everywhere at Christmastime. It was before the fear of offending others made most of them sadly disappear from parks and town squares. I remember taking a moment to look at one of these public Nativity scenes during a cold, December day. A snow was gently falling on each of the statues and even in the manger. About this time a mother walked up with her young son. The boy couldn't have been more than three years old. As they too stopped to stare at the beautiful sight the little boy removed his scarf and walked over to the Nativity. Then he folded it and placed it over the manger. He smiled as he walked back and said, "Baby Jesus looked cold." I thought that his mother would make him go back and retrieve the scarf, but thankfully she was made of wiser stuff than me at that time. She just smiled, wiped away a tear, and kissed her son on top of his head. Then leaving his gift of love, they slowly walked down the snow covered street together while the boy happily sang all the words he knew to "Silent Night."

It took a lot of years for me to grow as wise as that child, but when I did I realized that Christmas truly is about Love. It is about a love that is both joyfully shared and unconditional. It is about a love that sacrifices, cares, and gives. It is about loving each other just as much as God loves us at Christmastime and always.

Don't put the gift of Christmas up on some shelf on December 26th. Unwrap it and carry it in your heart all through the year.

THE GIFT

It was almost the middle of January and the snow had been on the ground since before Christmas. Storm after storm had hit us with no breaks in-between. Almost 6 feet of the white stuff had fallen in 6 weeks here. The bitterly cold temperatures had largely kept the snow from melting too. The arctic air had crept through the walls of my house and into my bones as well. All in all, it was the prefect recipe for a case of the Winter blahs.

To lighten my mood then I got out my old Christmas records that I had owned since I was a boy. I turned on the old record player I had bought at a yard sale a few years ago and put the needle to the vinyl. Soon the sweet sounds of "Silver Bells", "Silent Night", "Joy to the World", "Carol of the Bells", and "God Rest Ye Merry, Gentlemen" filled the air. Even the January snow looked more beautiful with "The Christmas Song" playing in the background. As I sang along I could feel the loving and joyous music heat up my heart and my home. It didn't matter that my home was no longer decorated, that there was no tree in the corner or presents under it, or that Christmas dinner had been replaced with hot dogs today. What mattered was that the gift of Christmas lived on inside of me. What mattered was that God's Love and Oneness filled my spirit not just on December 25th but every single day of my life.

Don't put the gift of Christmas up on some shelf on December 26th. Unwrap it and carry it in your heart all through the year. Its spirit will warm your Winter, brighten your Spring, make your Summer more special, and put even more Awe in your Autumn. It will remind you of God's unconditional love for you and help you to keep your own life focused on love as well. It will allow you to live everyday from your soul. And it will even allow you to sing the "Hallelujah Chorus" be it December, May, January, or June.

For me little miracles are the best kind.

BUTTERFLIES AND ANGELS

It is a funny thing how miracles come about. Everyone is always looking for some huge miracle to come out of the blue and save them when they are in a crisis, but they tend to ignore the little miracles that happen everyday right in front of their eyes. They call these little miracles luck or happen chance. I know what they really are, however. For me little miracles are the best kind.

So many of these little miracles happen around me all the time that I know that they are not just luck. One in particular has been happening a lot to me recently and it gives me a special joy. A few months ago I was telling my daughter some stories about my mom. My daughter was so young when my mom died that she doesn't remember her well. She relies on stories from dad to fill in the gap of not having her grandma here. I tell her all that I can remember of how wonderful my mom was and how much she meant to me. On one day a few months back my daughter was sad because her grandmother was in heaven now and she couldn't see her. I explained that even though grandma was an angel now she was still watching over us and could send us signs to let us know she was there. She could be anywhere she wanted to be even riding invisible on the back of a butterfly. Just after I said this a butterfly flew down right by me and my daughter and we laughed happily.

Now many people would say that was just luck that the butterfly flew down at that time. A funny thing, however, has happened since then. Every time I go out in any type of weather I see butterflies. Very often they fly right by my face to get my attention. I always say hi to mom when they do, send her my love, and thank God for little miracles which are the best kind.

As you go down the road of life remember that you are not alone. God and His angels are always with you.

A THOUSAND BUTTERFLIES

I have always loved butterflies. I think I must have got it from my Mom. When I was a boy she used to take a break from working in her flower garden just to watch these delicate winged beauties fly from blossom to blossom. After my Mom passed away I told my daughter many times that if her Grandma ever wanted to check up on her that she would probably just hop a ride on the back of a butterfly to do so. The amazing thing is that the more I would say it the more the butterflies would dance gracefully in the air around us when we walked outside. I would always smile and silently tell my Mom how much I loved her as they fluttered by.

This year I have seen more butterflies than ever before. I think my Mom must have gathered a thousand, invisible, angel riders to join her in watching over me. It is so glorious seeing all these butterflies floating on the breezes whenever I go out. I know that it is just my Mom's wonderful way of letting me know that she loves me, that she is looking out for me, and that she along with so many others are helping me as I travel down the road of my life.

It is so good to know that my Mom is still with me in my heart, mind, and soul. It is so blissful to feel her presence as I do my best to give love, spread joy, and make this world a better place. It is so wonderful to realize that a thousand angels are cheering me on as I strive to do what God wants me to do and go where God wants me to go. It is so peaceful knowing that this life I am living is a part of something far greater than myself.

As you go down the road of your life then always remember that you are not alone. God and His angels are always with you. They are watching you, helping you, and cheering you on as you love, give, and live. They are delighting in your every effort to do good and make this world a better place. And sometimes they are even riding unseen on back of a thousand butterflies.

God loves you so much. Why wait until you reach Heaven to be His angel?

ANGELS IN DISGUISE

I have been seeing so many more angels lately in my life that Earth is starting to seem a lot more like Heaven. Now by angels I am not talking about the ones in paintings with wings, halos, and robes. I am talking instead of those angels that love to hide behind a human form. They are what I joyously call angels in disguise.

These angels are everywhere. They hide in the bodies of your family, your friends, and the stranger you meet on the street. They greet you from behind the checkout counter and serve you dinner at your local restaurant. They look at you from behind the eyes of a ninety year old and a newborn infant. They come disguised as the rich, the poor, the vital, the sick, the healthy, and the handicapped. They smile at you from behind beautiful faces and genius intellects and also from within deformed bodies and disabled minds.

How can you tell who they are? It is simple. They are the ones who are radiating love to all those around them. They are the ones who are sharing joy with everyone they meet. They are the ones who are making the world a better place just by being in it. They are the ones who are giving us all a glimpse of Heaven while we are still here on Earth.

Do you want to know something wonderful? You can be an angel in disguise too. It is true despite your arguments to the contrary. Yes, you are a human being, but you are also a Child of God. Yes, you do live here on Earth, but the Kingdom of Heaven is within you. Yes, you have made a lot of mistakes in your life, but you can do a lot of good in it as well. Be an angel in disguise then. Look in the mirror and see the halo around your heart. Choose and share love and joy like an angel on Earth should. God loves you so much. Why wait until you reach Heaven to be His angel?

Angels do live among us. They surround us, guide us, protect us, and give us their beautiful example day after day.

I SAW AN ANGEL

I am pretty sure that I saw an Angel the other day. The halo wasn't there, but I am sure that it was hidden under the hat he had on. I couldn't see the wings either, but I am positive that they were covered up by the heavy coat he was wearing. I know the cane he walked with was just a part of the disguise as well. You can't expect an angel to just fly down the street in full glory without drawing some attention. Still, in spite of his ordinary clothes I am convinced that I saw an angel. The way he stooped down to pick up a package an elderly lady dropped was my first clue. The way he bent down to scratch a stray dog's head was further evidence of the fact. The clincher, though, was the way he beamed with a joyous smile as he gave something to a man collecting for charity and then wished him all the best with a voice that seemed to laugh and sing at the same time.

I wish this dear angel continued success in his chosen work of spreading love, joy, and light to the world. I know in my heart that the power of love and the goodness of God will be shared with everyone he meets. I know in my soul that there will be much singing, dancing, and rejoicing in Heaven with this blessed angel finally rejoins their midst. I know that my own heart and soul have grown stronger, better, and more loving for having seen him.

Angels do live among us. They surround us, guide us, protect us, and give us their beautiful example day after day. Some of them we can't see, but some of them walk right by us leaning on their canes and covered in their tattered old coats and hats. May all of us recognize them for who they are. May all of us follow their example. May all of us choose and share love and joy like these angels do.

Doing good and spreading joy can be as natural here on Earth as it is in Heaven.

YOUR INNER ANGEL

I saw another angel recently. Sometimes it is hard to spot them because they are so good at disguises. There was no white robe on this one. She was wearing a faded, flowered, sun dress not suited for the Winter weather. Her coat too was well worn and probably older than my grown up son. She didn't have a halo. Her white hair, though, sparkled when the light hit it and her smile shined with joy. There were no wings to be seen either. She was walking slowly in her scuffed up shoes while she pushed her shopping cart through the supermarket.

I knew that she was an angel, however, when at the checkout she divided her groceries into 3 small piles. She apologized to me for doing so but explained that she was buying food for two other elderly people who couldn't make it out in the bad weather. I just laughed and told her to take her time. It isn't everyday that you get to see an angel in action after all.

My ancient cherub squinted through her thick glasses and counted out the last of her change to pay for the groceries. Then she picked up her full bags and started to head out into the cold. She stopped for just a second though at a collection bin for the local humane society and quietly dropped in a bag of cat food and a bag of dog food. As I watched her walk into the swirling snow, I smiled and wondered if she was going to head for a car or fly up to Heaven.

That elderly angel in disguise reminded me once again to look for the inner angel in myself. She showed me one more time that doing good and spreading joy can be as natural here on Earth as it is in Heaven. She let me see that sharing God's love is not only easy to do, it is what we are meant to do. I hope then that all of you take the time today to find the inner angel inside yourselves. I hope that you let that angel out to bless the world with your love. And I hope that you always remember that you don't need wings to fly.

Smile back at all those special angels in disguise.

ANGEL SMILES

I have had a day full of angel smiles today and it isn't even noon yet. The one I got from the beautiful girl in the wheelchair made my whole morning brighter. It had a joy in it that flowed right from her lovely soul and into mine. The one I got from the baby boy in his Mother's arms was so sweet. It had only two teeth, but was accompanied with a waving hand and sparkling eyes that caused my own eyes to sparkle with delight as well. The one I got from the kind, old gentleman warmed my heart with its caring. It made his weathered and winkled face seem more handsome than any model's and reminded me that happiness can shine all the way to your last breath and your last smile. There were many others as well. It seemed like each person I passed today was a joyous angel in disguise with a smile to share with me. Each one made me smile even more myself until my soul was filled with peace and my heart sang with joy.

I am sure too that all the unseen angels around me were smiling this morning as well. I am sure that they were smiling when they saw the warmth, kindness, love, caring, and happiness that were passed along from smiling face to smiling face and from joyous soul to joyous soul. I am sure that they were smiling when they saw the light of God shining so brightly and being shared in so many lives this morning.

I hope that you have a glorious day full of angel smiles today and everyday of your life. I hope that you see the wonderful love, gentle caring, beautiful peace, and glorious joy behind each one of them. I hope too that you smile back at all those special angels in disguise. It is, after all, our love, our joy, our laughter, and our smiles that help us all to be Children of God and one with the angels.

There are many guardian angels in our lives. Some are unseen, but some walk with us and help us everyday.

GUARDIAN ANGELS

I believe in guardian angels. Since I was a boy I have felt watched over, loved, and protected by my unseen friends and I am so thankful to God for them. I have had far too many near misses with hurt and harm over the years for it to be mere luck. I guess my guardian angels are keeping me around for a reason and I will do my best not to make their work too hard in the future.

I also believe in guardian angels because I have seen one in action over the years. My oldest son graduates from high school this Spring. Through all of his years in school he has struggled with Autism. It has made it difficult for him to learn, to relate to others, and to function in this world. Thankfully, though, he has had a guardian angel with him every step of the way. His aide has been there with him through all the difficulties, through all the triumphs, through all the pains, and through all the joys. She was there when he first started to speak in sentences. She was there when he first started to read. She was there when he first started to make friends and play with the other children. She helped him through every frustration he faced and comforted him through every bit of sadness he had to endure. She helped him to become the happy and loving soul that he is today. She loved him, cared for him, guided him, encouraged him, and watched over him. She has been his aide, his friend, his second mother, and his guardian angel. Words can never express all the good that she has done for him. All I can say to her is "Thank you so much for being such an angel in my son's life."

There are many guardian angels in our lives. Some are unseen, but some walk with us and help us everyday. Take the time then to thank God for all the guardian angels in this world. Take the time as well to thank all the guardian angels that touch your own life. But most of all take the time to be a loving, joyous guardian angel yourself to every hurting heart that needs you.

God never fails to send us joyous angels and happy children to guide us back to love again.

CHILDREN AND ANGELS

I have often felt that children are far closer to the angels than we adults are. They seem far more ready to share joy freely and to give love unconditionally to others. They seem to easily know how to celebrate life, laugh, smile, and embrace delight just as God meant for all of us to do. Nothing brought this point home to my heart more clearly than a story a friend of mine recently shared with me about her daughter.

Her daughter while mentally handicapped has a soul that shines brighter than a thousand suns. She loves everyone and is never afraid to express her affection to others. Once when she was at Church with her Mom it came time to give others the sign of peace. Now most people do this with a handshake or a gentle touch. This little Angel Child, however, wasn't one to hold back on her love. She turned around and gave a sweet, elderly lady next to her a huge hug full of both energy and love. Later after Church that same lady with tears in her eyes approached the girl's Mom and spoke to her. "My husband just died a week ago", she said. "I felt so alone that I was going to go home and take some pills to end my life today, but now thanks to your little girl I believe that there still is love in this world."

Our children can teach us so much about love. Our children can teach us so much about joy. Our children can teach us so much about life. Let us not ignore the lessons they give us every day. Let us instead learn from them and share more love and joy with others in our own lives.

God loves us and put us here to love each other. Sometimes we forget this, but thankfully God is patient and forgiving with us. He never fails to send us joyous angels and happy children to guide us back to love again.

What would you do to make your guardian angels smile?

MAKE YOUR ANGELS SMILE

I read recently in an inspirational book that all of us have not just one guardian angel watching over us, but many such angels all though our days. This made me smile at the love God must have for us all to give us so much unseen help in our lives. It also made me feel a bit self-conscious about having angels watching over my every choice and action. In the end, however, I decided that I would just do my best moment by moment and day by day to make my guardian angels smile.

What would you do to make your guardian angels smile? Would you be polite to the person being rude to you and return kindness for anger and love for hate? Would you share part of the money you earn with those who are in great need and continue to trust in God to meet all your needs as well? Would you slow down your walk long enough to smell a newly blooming flower or freshly blossoming Cherry tree? Would you also stop to pick up a piece of trash littering the ground and make the world a bit more beautiful? Would you visit the sick, disabled, and elderly and give them not only your time but your joy and love as well? Would you sing out loud as you walk down the street and share your delight in being alive in spite of any looks others might give you? Would you hug your children and tell them how much you love them no matter how big they get or old they are? Would you bless this world with your smile, your kind words, your optimism, your enthusiasm, your laughter, your joy, your light, your talents, your energy, your cheerfulness, and your love? Would you do your best moment by moment, all though your day, and all though your life to be the person God meant for you to be?

I hope that all your answers were, Yes! I hope God and Heaven always look down on your life with joy and pride. And I hope that everyday you make your angels smile.

It is said that the eyes are the windows to the soul. It is good to know then that so many souls out there are full of light and willing to share that light with the world.

THE LIGHT IN YOUR EYES

Did you ever notice how people's eyes send out light? It is such an incredible thing to see. To look at that sparkling light coming out of someone's eyes always fills me with joy. I notice it shining especially in the eyes of happy little children, but I have seen it glowing just as brightly in the eyes of ninety year old's as well. Some people's eyes give out so much light that you can even see it in photographs of them. I feel so blessed when I see that light burning so brightly in the eyes of my wife, daughter, and two sons. It warms my heart and soul to see it and to feel their love and joy flowing through it.

It is said that the eyes are the windows to the soul. It is good to know then that so many souls out there are full of light and are willing to share that light with the world. When you look into another's eyes and see that light sparkling in joy it is easy to see how we are all Children of God and how much God loves each of us and wants us to love each other as well.

The next time you look in a mirror then notice the light in your own eyes. It is the same light that fills your soul and shines through your life. It is the light that God gave you and wants you to share with the world. Don't keep it hidden. Let it twinkle from your eyes, sparkle from your smile, and glow from your every loving act. Let it burn bright through your kind words, good deeds, helping hands, cheerful laughter, happy thoughts, and joyous life. Let that light within you out and help drive the darkness out of this world.

We all will one day die and the light will go out of our eyes. It won't disappear, though. It will just go home to the place where love, joy, and light never end and the light of God's love shines forever.

Look for the meaning of your life. It is there waiting for you in the depths of your heart and soul.

THE MEANING OF LIFE

What is the meaning of life? This is a question that has bothered saints and sinners and poets and philosophers since the beginning of mankind. It is a question that sooner or later is asked by each of us in our own lives. As I have grown a lot older and a tiny bit wiser, however, I have come to realize that this question has about 6 billion answers on Earth right now, because each of us has to find the meaning in our own life.

How can we do this? The great psychiatrist and survivor of the Nazi concentration camps, Victor Frankl said that we can find meaning in our lives in several ways. We can find it in what we do to make this world a better place. We can find it in the love that we give to other people. We can even find it in our pain, fear, suffering, and death when we use these things to become better, stronger, and more loving. It doesn't matter how long we live either because as Frankl says even a short life "could be so rich in joy and love that it could contain more meaning than a life lasting eighty years."

It took me a while, but I found the meaning in my own life. I found it in loving God, myself, my family, my community, and everyone in this world. I found it in sharing my love, joy, and oneness with God every second that I can today, tomorrow, and forever. I found it in showing the whole world that they can do the same through these simple words that I write.

What is the meaning of your life? Look for it. It is there waiting for you in the depths of your heart and soul. Then embrace it and spend the rest of your life living it. God gives each of us a purpose, a meaning, and a mission in our lives, and if we are still alive then we aren't done with them yet.

God has been, is now, and will always be LOVE!

I COULD NOT FIND IT

I just couldn't find it. I looked everywhere. I read through my Bible again and again. I looked in all the inspirational books I own. I checked out the other sacred texts as well. I walked through the woods looking for it. I even closed my eyes in meditation and prayer and looked for it deep within my own heart and soul. I could not find it anywhere. There was not a word, not a hint, and not even a feeling of it. Nowhere could I find a single drop of evidence that God is hate.

I know that a lot of people out there must think that God is hate. The protestors that hold up the signs about how God hates us at the funerals of miners and soldiers must think so. The people who say that earthquakes, tsunamis, and hurricanes are sent by God to punish us must think so. The terrorists who have killed thousands of innocent men, women, and children in their so called "holy war" must think so. As much as I tried, however, I couldn't find one single thing that supported their view.

I did find thousands of references to God's love in book after book. I found God's love in nature, in others, and in my own heart and soul. Every word I read, hint I found, and feeling I felt all said the same thing: "God is love." Maybe all of those who think that God is hate just aren't ready to know a God whose unconditional love is everywhere and in everyone. Maybe that is why they shut that love out. They want a God who loves little and hates much just like they do.

I just couldn't find that God anywhere I looked. I don't think I would ever want to either. I want the God who loves me and wants me to love as well. I want the God who fills every willing heart with love and joy. I want the God who has been, is now, and always will be LOVE.

I tried to count all the things I have to be thankful for, but I had to give up. There were just too many.

THINGS TO BE THANKFUL FOR

I tried to spend some time today counting all the things that I have to be thankful for, but I soon had to give up. There were just too many. I could not count them all even if I spent the rest of my life doing so. God loves us so much and showers us with so many blessings that it is impossible to number them. I ended up just saying, "Thank You God for my Life!"

I do, however, want to mention here just a few of the little things that I thought about today. Perhaps you are thankful for some of these same things yourself. Watching a bird fly across the sky while the sun goes down. The way the snow brightens the world on a cold winter's day. A cat sleeping peacefully on your lap. A dog who wants nothing more than to spend time with you. A family who gives you love and joy everyday of your life. Friends who touch your heart and warm your soul with their kindness. A hot cup of coffee and cold glass of orange juice in the morning. Delicious meals to eat. A warm bed to sleep in. A house that becomes a home from the love inside of it. Music that makes the heart sing, the eyes tear, and the spirit soar. Books full of words and ideas that not only enlighten the mind, but also touch the heart and uplift the soul. Trees, flowers, and animals that remind us daily that this is a beautiful world and that we should treat it with care. Fireflies sharing their light. Butterflies sharing their delight. Angels sharing their love. Laughter, smiles, singing, dancing, running, playing, and everything that brings us closer to joy. God's love all around us. God's love within us. God's love living through us. The miracle of life itself with all of its wonder, growth, and awe. The ability to choose love, the ability to share joy, and the ability to be who God made us to be.

May all of your days be full of blessings. May all of your days be full of happiness. May all of your days be full of thanks for all that we are given.

We need to hold our Father's hand and trust Him to lead us through this life and back home again.

KICKING AND SCREAMING

You can learn a lot from going to the market. The longer I live the more I learn just from going there with my eyes, ears, and heart open. The latest bit of wisdom that blessed me there came just the other day. A young mother was walking with her little child while pushing a cart loaded down with fruits and vegetables. The tiny toddler was complaining the whole time about how he hated all of these foods and wanted some candy. When his mother refused he began to throw a fit. His crying, kicking, and screaming were getting louder and louder until his mom firmly said, "If you don't behave and eat your fruits and vegetables then you won't be getting any of the homemade cookies your grandma brought over when we get home." With these words the crying stopped and the child's face brightened with an angelic smile. I could hear the pure delight in his voice when he said, "Oh Boy! Grandma made cookies."

I smiled then and realized that even as adults we are often like that toddler. God is holding our hands and leading us on a path of incredible growth in learning, goodness, love, and joy. The trouble is that often we are kicking and screaming all the way. We don't want what is really good for us. We want what we think will be good for us right now. We can't see those delicious, homemade cookies God has waiting for us, because we are too focused on that piece of hard candy in front of our eyes.

The rewards of love, joy, peace, happiness, goodness, and delight that God has waiting for us are far greater than we know. We just have to stop kicking and screaming and see that He is taking us where we need to go. We just have to enjoy our fruits and vegetables and know that even sweeter things are to come. We just have to hold our Father's hand and trust Him to lead us through this life and back home again.

God is showing us and telling us just how much He loves us everyday.

THAT IS GOD SAYING, "I LOVE YOU"

Each of us in this life wants more than anything to be loved. We work for love. We strive for love. We make fools out of ourselves for love. We long to feel that love warming our hearts and souls. We strain our ears each day for just a whisper of those three glorious words: "I love you."

What most of us don't realize, however, is just how much God loves us. God is showing us and telling us how much He loves us everyday. When you see the sun rising over the mountains, feel the cool breeze kissing your face, and hear the sweet songs of birds blessing your ears that is God saying, "I love you." When you see the adoring eyes of your dog looking up at you and feel the gentle brush of your cat against your hand that is God saying, "I love you." When you hear music that uplifts your soul with joy and read words that make your heart and mind soar into the heavens that is God saying, "I love you." When you hear the laughter of children playing and feel the warm hug of your own child against you that is God saying, "I love you." When you have the loving support of your family and the wonderful kindness of your friends no matter what you are going through that is God saying, "I love you." When you find your thoughts and feelings always leading you towards growth, learning, love, and joy that is God saying, "I love you." When your life's circumstances both good and bad help you to keep growing stronger, better, happier, and more loving each day that is God saying, "I love you."

God is always telling you and showing you just how much He loves you. Don't be afraid then to say, "I love you too God." Don't be afraid to live that love in your life either. Love God with everything you have and with everything you are. Love yourself, love your neighbor, and make this whole world your neighborhood. Always remember that God is love, that life is joy, and that we are one. And always listen for the million ways that God says, "I love you."

Don't make God have to tell you twice. Listen to Him the first time.

YOU DON'T HAVE TO TELL ME TWICE

An early April snow had caught us by surprise here in the mountains of my home. Flowers that had just popped out of the ground a week before were now drowning in a sea of white. It felt like someone had turned back the clock two months. Slowly it grew warm enough for the snow to begin to melt in the late afternoon but soon the temperatures dipped again as the cold, evening air turned the melted snow into ice.

Early the next morning I walked out to my cars. I needed to take my sons to school and then had a 30 mile round trip to make after that. I wondered which car to take. My little one had the better gas mileage, but the tires on my bigger one were less worn. Just as I took a step towards my little car, however, my foot slipped on a patch of black ice and I felt my body hitting the driveway. I got up slowly and smiled. "You don't have to tell me twice God!", I said before heading over to start the car with the better tires. After dropping off my boys at school I made the round trip safely. I felt my car hit patches of black ice several times, but each time the tires gripped and adjusted well. I found myself laughing and grinning even with my still sore left hip and shoulder. I was happy I had followed God's guidance and I felt loved and watched over.

God's loving guidance comes in many ways. You can hear its gentle whisper in your heart. You can listen to it come out in the touching lyrics of a beautiful song. You can see it in the wise passage of a book. You can notice it in an overheard scrap of conversation. You can feel it in the quietness of nature. You can even get it when you fall to the pavement of your driveway. However it comes to you, though, don't turn away from it. Don't make God have to tell you twice. Listen to Him the first time. Trust Him, love Him, and follow Him. He will take you to ever greater love, joy, and learning. He will keep you safe and lead you home.

The next time you catch the moon smiling at you, smile back and thank God for all the wonderful reminders of His love.

REMINDERS OF HIS LOVE

Have you ever noticed when you are walking outside on the night of a crescent moon that if you turn your head sideways that the moon seems to be smiling at you? It is just another one of the countless reminders all around us of God's love for us.

God's love for us is everywhere and in everything. The reminders of it are like a shower of joy that we get every time we walk outside our homes or look inside ourselves. They range from a little baby with joyous shining eyes smiling at you in a grocery store to a delightful chorus of birdsong greeting you when you go out to get a morning paper to a beautiful sunrise and glorious sunset to start and end each day. They vary from a loving hug from a happy child to a soul touching passage from a book to a glorious piece of music that uplifts your heart on angel wings. They differ from a crystal snowfall on the first day of Winter to blooming flowers just outside your window to kind words that remind you that you are a Child of God and worthy of His love.

Why does God give us all these reminders of His love for us? Why does God shower us with so much goodness, love, joy, and delight? Perhaps it is because God wants us to be happy and share love as well. When you know just how much God loves you and when you see just how much joy accepting and sharing that love brings then finally all of your life makes sense and you want to share that love and joy with everyone everywhere.

God loves us all so much. God gives us so many reminders of that love everyday. The least we can do then is accept that glorious and powerful love into our hearts and souls and share it with the rest of the world. The next time you catch the moon smiling at you then, smile back and thank God for all the wonderful reminders of His love.

In this life we are all students and we are all teachers. What we learn and what we teach, however, is up to us.

PROFESSOR OF LIFE

When I was in college I had a professor who taught me a lot not only about English, but also about life. He taught with a joy, energy, and enthusiasm that touched everyone in his classes. He made us laugh, he made us learn, and he made us think as well. Here are just a few of the things that he taught me. He taught me that work isn't about getting a paycheck at the end of each week, it is about loving what you do and doing what you love. He taught me not to take life so seriously and that laughter is good when facing life's difficulties. He showed me that life is best when lived with zest and vitality and that what you put into life is what you get back from it. He showed me that the school of life is never out and that we keep learning everyday of our lives. He explained how everything from music, to books, to people, to experiences can be our teachers if we are only willing to learn. He explained too that it is always best to learn with enthusiasm and to live with joy.

I was truly blessed to have had such a great teacher at such a young age. He opened my mind and started me on the path of a lifetime's worth of learning. I have tried to stay a good student of life since then. I have also tried to be a decent teacher as well by passing on what I have learned in my writings and in my life. Only time will tell how good a one I have been.

In this life we are all students and we are all teachers. What we learn and what we teach, however, is up to us. May you always learn in enthusiasm and in joy then. May you always teach with energy and with love as well. May you never stop learning what God needs you to learn and may you always teach what God wants you to teach. I hope that you graduate this life with honors as a Child of God and I hope that you spend all of your years here as a Professor of love and of life.

We can choose to be the person God meant for us to be.

DREAM CATCHERS

On the wall above my bed there are two very beautiful dream catchers that my wife bought. They are red and brown willow hoops decorated with feathers, horse hair, and beads. They have a wonderfully delicate, spider web design in the middle of them. At the very center of the web in the very middle of the dream catcher there is a round hole. The Native American Lakota Tribe believes that the dream catchers represent the web of life. Their people believe that hanging them above your bed or in your house will sift your dreams and visions. The good in your dreams will be caught in the web and carried with you, but the evil in your dreams will pass through the hole and no longer be a part of your life.

I enjoy looking at these lovely dream catchers, because they always remind me of what I want to do in my own life. I want to catch only the good within myself. I want to capture only the highest, wisest, best, most loving, most giving, and most joyous part of myself and let the rest fade away. I want to become the person that God meant for me to be and live the way that God meant for me to live. I want to become a wonderful part of the web of life and share only love and joy with others and the world.

The glorious truth is that you, I, and everyone else in this world can do this too. God loves us all so much and God gives us the strength and ability to become our highest selves. We can choose to be the person God meant for us to be. We can fill ourselves with love, joy, and light and then share them with the world. We can capture the angel within and allow the worst parts of ourselves to fade away. We can live as a true Child of God sending smiles, giving love, offering joy, scattering sunshine, and creating laughter wherever we go. We can catch the dream of the person we always wanted to be and make it a reality.

Take your little light then and let it shine.

THIS LITTLE LIGHT OF MINE

"This little light of mine, I'm gonna let it shine." I have always loved that song ever since I was a little boy. I was listening to it again today as my wife and I were babysitting our friend's two little girls. I could even see the light shining from the eyes of the eight month old baby and her three year old sister as they giggled, played, and smiled at me. It was such a beautiful light so full of joy, bliss, happiness, and delight. It was such a glorious light so full of miracles, magic, goodness, and love. It was a light that reached right down into my soul and reminded me once again what we are here on Earth for: to love, care for, help, and rejoice in each other.

I don't know why so many people refuse to shine their light. I don't know why so many other people even try to dim and cover the shining lights of those around them. All that I do know is that each of us has a light within us. We have it from the day we are born until the day we die. We carry it within our souls all through this life and on into the next. It is the light of love and it is given to us by a God who loves us more than we will ever know. We can let it flicker and go out or we can nurture it, feed it, and let it shine its glorious light to the whole world.

Take your little light then and let it shine. Let it shine from your eyes and light up your smile. Let it glow through your countless loving acts of caring, goodness, and compassion. Let it burn from your heart and ignite the heart lights of all those you meet. Let it be a beacon of joyous delight from your soul to the entire world. God gave you a wondrous, beautiful light called love. Don't let it grow dim. Choose it, share it, spread it, give it, and let it shine, let it shine, let it shine.

If all of us were to add even more goodness to what we already have received and then pass it on, the world would become a Heaven on Earth.

DOING GOOD

I love doing good things for people. It brightens my day, brings joy to my heart, and makes me feel closer to God. They say that loving and doing good are their own rewards. It is true too. Even if you get no external rewards for doing something good the inner joy and satisfaction you feel are more than enough. That is why I enjoy doing good in secret so much. Knowing that I have no chance of being rewarded for my actions makes my inner joy all the sweeter.

I think that all of us need to remember that the true rewards of doing good happen within ourselves. Far too many people expect to be rewarded by others for every good thing they do. They even stop doing good things when the rewards aren't there. All of us need to do good expecting nothing in return. To expect a reward takes away from the joy and satisfaction you feel inside. It also robs your act of its goodness. To do good only for a reward makes the act a selfish one rather than a giving one.

People, of course, do like to reward us when we do good. There is nothing wrong with receiving thanks for the good things you have done. It brings both you and those thanking you great joy. Another good thing that you can do, however, is to encourage others who wish to repay your goodness to pass it on instead. If all of us where to pass on the goodness we received in this life, the world would be full of joy. If all of us were to add even more goodness to what we have already received and then pass it on, the world would become a Heaven on Earth.

Do good things for people then. Give goodness and joy to everyone without expecting anything in return. Receive goodness from others happily and then with a loving heart pass it on as well. We can make this world the Paradise of Goodness God meant for it to be if we choose.

It doesn't matter how tiny a candle you may think your life is, you can still use it to shine a little light and love in this world.

A TINY CANDLE

Many people have said that our lives on this Earth are just brief sparks of light that make little difference in the grand scheme of things. I have heard countless times how a single human life is just a tiny candle in the darkness of the world. Still, I remember as a boy in 4-H camp how at the final council circle we were all given a single tiny candle. These candles by themselves were nothing, but as one candle was used to light another the council circle grew less dark. Then as each lit candle was used to light still others the council circle began to glow with a wonderful brightness. In the end as every single candle was lit the council circle was bathed in a glorious, shining light of not only fire but love and joy as well.

It doesn't matter how tiny a candle you may think your life is then. You can use it to shine a little light and love in this world. It doesn't matter how briefly your candle flickers. It can still be used to light other candles and spread love and joy to them. It doesn't matter how small your flame burns right now. You can feed it and build it and watch it grow. You may think that your life is a tiny candle now, but you can make it into a mighty bonfire if you choose. Then all those whose lives are still tiny unlit candles can light themselves from your powerful light and love.

Light your candle today. Place it gently to the roaring fire of love and joy that God has built for us all. Watch it burn brightly and warmly. Then extend it to the unlit candles all around you. Share your loving, joyous fire with everyone you know and everyone you meet. Feed your fire with goodness and God and watch it cast out all the darkness of the world. Spread all the love, joy, and light you can and your flame will forever burn bright.

Each of us has a beautiful song within ourselves just waiting to be sung. Don't go to your grave with your song still inside of you.

YOU HAVEN'T HEARD ANYTHING YET

I talked to my Aunt on the phone again today. I always feel so much better after hearing her gentle voice. Her contagious laughter, kind words, and unconditional love always uplift my soul and always bring me so much happiness. She is such a blessing to me, her children, her grandchildren, her friends, her church, her community, and everyone that she meets. She has more energy, vitality, and joy at 80 than most people have at 20. She does more good, spreads more cheer, and touches more hearts than I could ever hope to. She is still singing the sweet song of her life, and its beautiful and joyous music continues to touch the hearts and souls of all who hear it.

I only hope that my life's song can one day be half as beautiful as hers'. I know one thing for sure, however. I will never stop singing it. I will sing it with all my heart whether I live another 4 days or another 40 years. Walt Whitman once wrote: "The strongest and sweetest songs yet remain to be sung." I want my own life's song then to grow stronger in joy and sweeter in love each and everyday. I want my own life's song to reach the ears, hearts, and souls of everyone I meet. I want my own life's song to spread God's love and Heaven's music for all of my days.

Each of us has a beautiful song within ourselves just waiting to be sung. Don't go to your grave with your song still inside of you. Start singing it today. Let it flow from your heart, soul, and life. Let it bring your sweet music to the world. Let it bring the notes of your love, joy, and oneness with God to everyone you meet. Let it fill the air with every good thing that is within you. Then when someone comes up to you and asks you how your life is going you can honestly say, "You haven't heard anything yet!"

A house is a building you buy. A home is a place full of love.

A HOUSE OR A HOME

I was on the phone with my Aunt the other day telling her about my latest misadventure in fixing up my house. My attempts at home improvement often end up looking more like attempts in home destruction. As I was relating my latest home repair mistake, however, my loving Aunt in her gentle and humorous wisdom reminded me that I live in a home not a house.

My Aunt was right, of course. A house never brings warm memories to your heart. A house provides neither comfort nor security. A house is a building you buy not a place you love. A home on the other hand is a place that is full of love. A home is a place to feel relaxed and at peace. A home is a place to create countless happy memories. A home is a place where you live not just exist. I have been so blessed to have lived in homes rather than houses. I am so grateful for the wonderful memories I have of my childhood homes, of visiting my Aunt's home in the Summer, and of raising my own children in my own home.

My home right now may be a little worn down. It may appear "lived in" no matter how much I clean it. It may never look picture perfect. Still, I wouldn't trade it for the world. My home is a place of love, joy, peace, and happiness. I would always rather live in a home instead of a house. I would always rather make my life a home instead of a house.

What kind of place and what kind of life are you going to live in? Are you going to choose a house with its cleanness, order, efficiency, and coldness or are you going to choose a home with its love, laughter, happiness, and warmth? May you choose wisely and may God bless your home and your life always.

The road of live may be curvy, but every twist and turn in it can lead you to greater love and joy.

A CURVY ROAD

There are a lot of curves in the roads around my home. It has never been easy to drive into a mountain, so the roads here twist, turn, go up and then down. It can be confusing to an out of state driver who is used to being able to see for miles ahead. For those of us who grew up here, though, it is nothing to worry about. We know that even if we can't see what is around the next curve that the road will still take us where we need to go.

Life is a lot like these roads that I drive on everyday. Life is full of curves, twists, and turns. Sometimes it seems like the uphill climb will last forever and then suddenly you find yourself coasting downhill and enjoying the view. You can't always see beyond the next curve to what lies ahead, but still you have to trust that God will lead you to where you need to go.

I know that my own life has taken more curves than I ever thought it would. It has twisted and turned in ways that I would never have planned and yet it has taken me to right where I needed to be. Along the way I have been carsick more than once, but I have also seen wonderful beauty, experienced great learning, and met many fellow travelers who have helped me to grow in love and joy. I am still traveling on my life's curvy road and I still have a long way to go. I am confident, however, that God will use it to take me home.

As you travel on your own road of life don't be scared. The road may be curvy, but every twist and turn in it can lead you to greater love and joy if you let it. Travel this road with a smile on your face, laughter in your heart, and a song in your soul and know that God will see to it that this road leads you home.

In God's eyes there are no lepers only children needing and deserving love.

THE YOUNG MAN AND THE LEPER

There is a story from the Middle Ages that has always touched my heart. The grown son of a rich merchant was walking down the road towards his home after visiting friends. As he neared a curb he heard the ring of a leper's bell coming from the other way. At that time Leprosy was a highly contagious, incurable disease. Lepers were not allowed in the towns and were forced to ring bells to warn others as they walked the roads. Before the young man could leave the road the leper rounded the curb and was suddenly face to face with him.

The leper's face and body had become horribly disfigured by the disease and when the young man saw him he drew back in disgust. As the leper lowered his head and began to walk on, however, the young man felt his heart breaking for the man. He quickly caught up to the leper and apologized for how he had acted. Then he gave the leper all the money he was carrying and hugged him. The leper looked at the young man with tears in his eyes and said that was the first time anyone had touched him in many years. That blessed moment began a change in the young man's heart and started him on a different path that would also affect the whole world. You see, that young man would later become Saint Francis of Assisi.

There are many types of "lepers" in our modern world that could use our love, help, and hugs. The homeless, sick, poor, disabled, elderly, and mentally handicapped often have to wear the "bells" that society forces on them. Many of them go through life either avoided or looked down upon. Like that young man, though, we can make a difference in their lives with just one gesture of caring and love. Like him we can let God's love shine through us to touch their hearts and souls. And we may also find as he did that their love can touch and change us for the better as well. Remember, in God's eyes there are no lepers only children needing and deserving love.

God never stops forgiving us. Why should we ever stop forgiving others?

FORGIVENESS

I was driving down the road the other day when I saw a sign in front of a church. It said, "Forgive your enemies. It messes with their minds." As I read this sign I felt a smile come to my lips, a feeling of delight come to my heart, and a long, deep laugh come from my belly. When I finally stopped laughing at the joyous humor on this sign I realized something. What it said couldn't be more true.

A person whose mind is full of anger, after all, gives anger to the world and expects anger in return. In the same way a person whose heart is full of hate, shares that hate with the world and expects hate in return. Likewise a person whose soul is full of hurting passes that hurt on to the world and expects to be hurt again in return. It is a horrible and vicious cycle that eventually destroys the person's life and harms everyone he touches.

It is forgiveness that breaks this cycle, however. It is forgiveness that messes up the mind full of anger and shows it that there is another way to live. When you forgive another you keep your own mind full of peace, your own heart full of love, and your own soul full of joy. When you forgive another you pass these precious gifts along to them as well. When you forgive another you live the way that God meant for you to live and you show everyone around you how a Child of God can make this world a better and more loving place.

Keep on forgiving others then. Keep on messing with their minds. Keep on helping their hearts and souls. Keep on living the life that God meant for you to live. If you have to do it seventy times seven times then do so happily. God never stops forgiving us. Why should we ever stop forgiving others?

Kindness always ripples out and travels from person to person until it circles the world and returns home to the heart that first shared it.

ACTS OF KINDNESS

I can remember several years ago a wonderful, November morning at my son's elementary school. I had just taken him into the special education room where he started each morning. The teacher and aides were talking about how much my son and the other students had enjoyed some chocolate donuts that they had been given for a snack the week before. I chatted with them for a few minutes and left. As I walked though the parking lot, however, a wonderful, kind thought came into my mind. I always try to follow such thoughts too, because I learned long ago that any thought full of love and kindness usually comes right from God.

Wrapping my winter coat around me then I headed straight for the local grocery store and bought two boxes of donuts, one for my son and his friends and the other for the teacher and aides that always took care of them with so much love, kindness, and compassion. Hurrying back I was able to deliver my simple gift before the start of school. The smiles on the faces I saw paid me back a hundred times over and I walked out smiling myself with a warmer heart and a lighter soul. I had paid little in the way of time or money, but that God inspired act of kindness had purchased more joy, goodness, and delight than I could have ever dreamed possible.

A little act of kindness goes a long way towards making this world a better place. Each kind thing we do connects us to the hearts, souls, and lives of those around us. Each kind word we say and kind thought we think brings us closer to love, closer to each other, and most importantly closer to God. Kindness always ripples out as well and travels from person to person until it circles the world and returns home to the heart that first shared it. May you always fill your life with kindness then. May all your days be full of loving thoughts, joyous feelings, and kind acts. May you always make the world a kinder place just by being in it.

I want to spend all my days living and not dying.

LIVING NOT DYING

"I'll be living when I die." I read those beautiful and wise words today in a story a friend sent me. They rang so true to my heart and soul that I found myself repeating them all day long. They made me think again of how I really want to live my life to the fullest every single day. They made me think again of how silly it is to think and worry about death when there is so much living to do in this life. They made me think again of how I want to continue to grow in and share love and joy, day by day and year by year, so that my very last day can be my very best day as well. They made me think again of how much caring, giving, helping, laughing, hugging, singing, dancing, smiling, and loving goes into truly living.

I want to spend all my days living and not dying. I want to spend all my days taking in the wonders of a sunset, smelling the sweetness of flowers, and rejoicing in the love of my family. I want to spend all my days choosing joy, sharing joy, and showing others that they can do the same. I want to spend all my days doing all that I can to make this world a better, more beautiful and more wonderful place to live in.

Leo Buscaglia said in one of his speeches that he wanted his tombstone to read: "Here lies Felice Leonardo Buscaglia who lived himself to death." May all of us be able to say the same. May all of us when we face God at the end of our lives be able to say that we truly lived and truly loved. May all of us be able to smile with our last sigh. May all of us be able to laugh and not cry when death knocks at our door, because we lived our lives to the fullest and gave all that we were to the world. May all of us be able to say from the bottom of our hearts and the depths of our souls, "I'll be living when I die."

We are meant for joy. It is our birthright.

JOY

The great Leo Buscaglia once told a story about what the ancient Egyptians believed about the afterlife. They believed that they would be asked two questions that would determine whether or not they could continue their journey into paradise. The first was, "Did you find joy?" and the second was, "Did you bring joy?" If you ask me those two questions still apply today.

We humans, after all, are meant for joy. It is our birthright. If we can't find a thousand things each day to be joyful about and grateful for then we are probably not living our lives as fully and as openly as we could. If we can't find countless ways each day to bring joy into our lives and the lives of others then we are probably not living the way God meant for us to live. God loves us all and wants more than anything for us to be joyous in this life we are given. We are here to learn to love. We are here to choose love, to share love, and to give love without expecting anything in return. We are here to fill our heart to overflowing with love. And Love is Joy!

Make sure then that when you do pass from this world that you can answer a definite Yes! to both questions. Look to find joy where ever you go and in whatever you do. See it shining in a baby's smiling face. Hear it in the musical laughter of children. Find it in family, friendship, learning, books, music, nature, and animals. Recognize it in every hug you receive, kind word you hear, and miracle you are blessed with. Notice it in the smiling man in the moon and the robin splashing in your birdbath. Fill yourself full of this God-given joy and then bring it to the world. Share God's joy through your smile, kindness, laughter, goodness, caring, giving, helping, and loving. Make this world a better place because of the joy you found and shared.

Give your smile away today, but don't be surprised if you find it returned back to you again and again.

THE GIFT THAT KEEPS ON RETURNING

I have a gift that I just can't seem to give away. Every time I try to give it to someone I get it returned. I gave it to my Dad the other day and he went and gave it right back. I tried to give it to both my sons and daughter this morning, but they wouldn't keep it either. They gave it back to me almost immediately. I tried to pass it on to a few friends that I saw when I took my children to school, but they refused to accept it and passed it back to me again. Later on I saw my neighbor and offered it to her. She gave it back even quicker than everyone else. Finally I even decided to try and give it to all the strangers I passed on the street and in the stores. A few of them looked like they might take it without passing it back to me, but in the end every single person returned it.

I looked at it in the mirror this afternoon wondering what was wrong with it and why noone would keep it. It seemed like such a beautiful, wonderful, joyous, and God given gift. In the end I guessed that a gift this good couldn't be hoarded and had to keep traveling on from heart to heart and soul to soul. It was no wonder then that I kept getting my smile returned every time I tried to give it away.

I hope that all of you give your smile away today. Don't be surprised, however, if you find it returned back to you again and again. A gift of such beauty, joy, peace, love, and delight is a gift from God and it travels back and forth connecting hearts, souls, minds, and lives. It is a simple gift that takes so little effort and yet brings such goodness to this world. Its value is beyond compare. It enriches the lives of those who receive it and also the lives of those who give it away. It is the gift that keeps on returning and the gift that blesses us all our lives long.

Laughter often goes hand in hand with both love and joy.

LAUGH

I find myself laughing a lot more these days. It isn't a mean laughter that hurts others' feelings, either. It is rather a laughter of wonderful delight that makes my heart feel light, my body feel great, and my soul feel pure joy. It is a laughter that comes when things go right and when things go wrong. It is a laughter that finds humor and bliss in all the ups and downs of life. It is a laughter that comes from loving God, loving life, loving myself, and loving others.

I think that laughter often goes hand in hand with both love and joy. When we choose love and when we choose joy, we also choose laughter. This is because when we love God, ourselves, and others we can't help but feel joyous. And when we feel joyous we can't help but share it with the world through wondrous and delightful laughter. I think that God must often laugh in delight too as He watches over us with loving eyes and a joyous smile

Don't be afraid to laugh. Don't hold it back. Let it out. Let it fill your heart, soul, mind, and voice. Let it brighten your day. Let it travel from you to all those around you and fill the air with its sweet, joyous music. William Blake once wrote "The Angel that presided at my birth said: 'Little creature, formed of joy and mirth, Go, love without the help of anything on earth.'"

Let's all make the angels that watch over us and the God who made us smile with delight at our lives then. Let's all choose to love each other, share joy with each other, and laugh together. Let's all laugh all through the day, at every chance we get, and at everything that brings humor and delight into our lives. Let's laugh at the puppy chasing her tail, at the baby giggling at our funny faces, and at the countless silly things we say and do. Let's laugh at the problems life gives us and the good times life brings us. Let's always live our lives with laughter, love, and delight.

No matter how much love you give to others or joy you share with them, you always end up with more than you started with.

EVER INCREASING JOY

One of the most fascinating discoveries that I have made in my life is that no matter how much love you give to others or joy you share with them you still end up with more than you started with. It is a wonderful miracle that never stops amazing me. When I smile and wave at my neighbor across the road I send all of my joy with it. Yet, when I go back inside my house I find that I have even more joy warming my heart and soul than I did before. When I stop to share a few nice words with someone I meet I share my kindness with them as well. Later, however, I find that the kindness in me has grown greater rather than less. When I give my children a hug and tell them I love them I can actually feel the love flowing from my heart and soul to their's. Still, when I look inside myself afterwards I find that the love within me has increased once again.

I still smile everyday at this wonderful miracle although it must drive the mathematicians crazy. I rejoice in this special law of giving that God has blessed our hearts and souls with. I thank God for the ever increasing joy, love, peace, happiness, goodness, and delight that flows back into my life whenever I share it with others. I hope too that one day the entire world realizes this glorious truth and lives it as well.

Norman Vincent Peale said, "Joy increases as you give it, and diminishes as you try to keep it for yourself." Never stop giving your joy away then. Never stop sharing your love with the world. You will be amazed at just how much love you can bless others with. You will be delighted at just how much joy you can spread. And most of all you will be surprised at just how much more love and joy grows in your heart and soul when you do so.

An empty lap is far less happy than one that has a cat, dog, or young child sitting on it.

LITTLE LESSONS

Everyday life has taught me a lot of things over the years. It has filled me with hundreds of little lessons that have brought so much laughter into my life, love into my heart, and joy into my soul. Here are just a few of the many wonderful bits of wisdom that life has given me.

When raking leaves in the backyard always rake them into a big pile. This makes it easier for you and your children to jump and play in them. Shoveling snow off the driveway isn't complete until you make a snow angel, build a snowman, and have at least one snowball fight. When mowing the lawn always leave a clump of dandelions or sweet clover standing for the butterflies to enjoy. You will get tired of playing fetch long before your dog does, but you should still play anyway. An empty lap is far less happy than one that has a cat, dog, or young child sitting on it. A clean house isn't always a happy house. The best homes look lived in, laughed in, and loved in. It is hard to give away a smile. It almost always gets returned to you. Arms are meant for hugging, hands are meant for holding, and lives are meant for living. You can't give too much love or share too much joy. The more love you give to others the more love you have in your heart. The more joy you share with others the more joy you have in your soul. If you are too busy to watch a sunset, play with your kids, read a book, listen to music, or gaze at the stars then you are just too busy period. We can create Heaven on Earth or we can create Hell on Earth. It is our choice. I much prefer Heaven on Earth myself.

One last thing that I have learned is that God loves us more than we will ever know and that God wants us to be happy in our lives. Why else would we be down here learning these little lessons about life, love, and joy? I hope that you have a lifetime of happiness learning yours and sharing them with others.

God put us here to make beautiful music with our lives.

WIND CHIMES

I am listening to some beautiful music right now. Just hearing it brings joy to my soul and a smile to my face. It wasn't written by any songwriter though. This music was written by God Himself and carried with His love on the winds right into my heart. This music comes from the wind chimes on my back porch. They are ringing with delight at every gust of the warm, March wind that is blowing outside my home right no. Their every chime, ring, and tingle sings with joy and makes wonderful music as they dance with the swirling winds of nature.

I have always loved wind chimes even as a little boy. I have always delighted in the peaceful, loving music they bring. I even have a tiny set given to me by my loving wife hanging in my car. I find their gentle song soothing to my soul whenever I listen to them.

The thing that amazes me most about wind chimes, however, is that no matter which way the wind blows or how hard the gusts hit them, they still sing. They sing their songs and make their music on warm, sunny days like today and on dark, cold, rainy days as well. They delightfully ring to greet the rising sun and still tingle during the darkest night. They bring forth their joyous sounds when surrounded by others and also when noone else is around. If we all could just follow their example what glorious music we could fill this world with.

Don't ever let your own music die inside you. Don't ever hold your own chimes silent. God put us here to make beautiful music with our lives. God put us here to make each of our days a song of love, laughter, joy, delight, caring, and sharing. Let your own chimes sing always then. Make your own life a concert of joy no matter which way the winds may turn you.

We are Children of God letting His peace, love, and joy come through our every thought, feeling, and action.

WHO WE REALLY ARE

I heard the sweetest, most beautiful, and most delightful sound the other day. It warmed my heart, brought a smile to my lips, and filled my soul with joy when I heard it. It was the glorious sound of children laughing, playing, running, and singing. It was beautiful music to my ears and a wonderful reminder of who we really are in this life.

All too often I think we forget who we really are in this life. We get so caught up in our struggles, conflicts, hatreds, judgements, and troubles that we stop seeing who we really are and why we are really here. We get so wrapped up in the pain, fear and darkness that are sometimes in this life that we forget the joy, love, and light that dwells within each of our hearts and souls.

Who are we really then? We are more than just these bodies that we walk around in. We are more than just these random thoughts that fill our minds. We are more than just the reactions and feelings that come upon us all day long. We are instead glorious creations of God capable of so much goodness, peace, and happiness. We are spreaders of delight to sad minds. We are sharers of joy to lonely hearts. We are givers of love to weakened souls. We are magical human beings creating smiles and laughter wherever we go. We are angels in disguise giving messages of God's love to everyone in the world. We are beings of light casting out the darkness of the world with our bright, shining souls. We are Children of God letting His peace, love, and joy come through our every thought, feeling, and action. We are miracles of life and love making the world a better place just by being in it. We are wondrous souls living the way we were meant to live. We are all these things and even more. It is up to us, however, to remember who we really are and why we are really here. It is up to us to be what God always meant for us to be.

You won't need any pockets for the clothes you are buried in.

WHAT YOU CAN TAKE WITH YOU

    I stopped at a local convenience store the other day to fill up my gas tank before heading back home. After pumping the gas I headed in, grabbed a pack of gum, and got in line to pay. In the front of the line was a tired looking woman, holding a toddler in her arms. Behind her and just in front of me was an older man with white hair and a white shirt. He smiled kindly at me and patiently waited while the woman struggled to hold her child while she counted out change with her free hand. She searched twice in her pocket book but still didn't have enough money to pay for the two gallons of milk she had brought to the counter. I could see her lips tremble and her eyes moisten as she apologized and picked up one of the gallons to take back.
    It was then that the older man stopped her. With a gentle smile he told the cashier that he would pay for the milk. The look of relief on the poor woman's face touched my heart. She thanked the older man while he smiled again and said not to worry about it. As she exited the store I could see that her eyes were still moist, but this time the tears were for a different reason. As he paid for her milk and his own items the white haired angel in disguise smiled at me one last time. Then as he was walking out of the store he gave me a wink and said, "You can't take it with you, you know."
    What he said is true. You won't need any pockets for the clothes you are buried in. Every dime you have made in this world has only been a loan for you to use for a short time. Still, there are a few things that the white haired gentleman and all of us will be taking with us when we do go to our final home. Every look of relief that we bring to another will go with us as will every bit of love we share and kindness we do. Every moment of learning and joy will come with us as well. And every smile that we bring to God's face will be waiting for us there too.

You may just be one voice among many, but if your share your soul's song you can add so much to the choir.

PART OF THE CHOIR

When I was a boy our church didn't have a choir so everyone was expected to sing. That didn't bother me since I was an enthusiastic singer to say the least. Still, my talent didn't quite match my zest for singing. More often than not I was too loud and off key. Many times my singing would get me a nudge and a look from my older brother. In time, though, I learned to sing more softly and found that even my less than perfect voice blended in beautifully with the choir of joyous singers that was our church.

As I grew up too I found many other ways to sing my soul's song without using my throat's voice. One way was by putting a pen to paper and later my fingers to a keyboard. In this way I was able to share the inspiring thoughts, words, and experiences that my Heavenly Father so often gave me. In this way I was able to encourage others as well to choose love, share joy, and grow in oneness with God even as I learned to do so more and more in my own life.

As the years have gone by too I have realized something. I am only one voice in millions out there writing, speaking, and singing out the beautiful truth for all the world to hear. I often see the others online, in newspapers, on television, in books, and even on the street. Some have become rich and famous for the work they have done, but most like me are just delighting in freely sharing the wisdom, joy, love, and light that God has given them.

Now I find myself happy to be a part of a new choir that is doing all it can to bring the glorious music of love to this world. I hope that you will join it as well. You may be just one voice among many, but if you share your soul's song you can add so much to the choir. It doesn't matter either if your voice or life is less than perfect. If you sing your song and live your life with love, you can help to make the Earth sound a lot more like Heaven.

I have realized that you can't go through life being afraid to die and you can't go through life being afraid to live.

NOT AFRAID TO DIE

Somewhere along this journey of life something amazing happened: I stopped being afraid to die. I am not sure when it happened exactly, but the fear of death is no longer with me. I think it happened gradually over the years. Part of me began to see death not as the enemy but as a reminder. It was a reminder to me that I didn't have forever on this world and that I needed to live everyday to the fullest. I also began to realize more and more over the years just how much God loves each and everyone of us in this life. I began to feel that love in my heart and soul and know that God has a wonderful plan for us all in this life and in the next. Finally, I began to love life itself more and more. As that love of life grew my fear of death shrank. I knew that life was too glorious and beautiful to simply be limited to this world. I knew that even greater life and even greater love must await us beyond it.

Being unafraid to die doesn't mean, however, that I have grown foolhardy or careless in my life. If anything it has made me appreciate and rejoice in this life I have been given even more. I still look both ways when I cross the street and wear a seatbelt in my car. I am no longer afraid, though, to smile at strangers or to stop to help someone in need. I have realized that you can't go through life being afraid to die and you can't go through life being afraid to live.

Give up your fears. They only serve to block your love. Be unafraid to die and be unafraid to live. Trust in God. Fill yourself with His love, joy, and light. Go through life living and loving as if each day were your last. Go through life sharing joy, creating delight, and doing good fearlessly. Go through life knowing in your heart, soul, and mind that there is no death only never-ending life.

Losing my Mom when I was so young did teach me one thing: we don't have forever in this world. If we want to share our love and joy with others then we have to do so now.

MOM

The holidays have always been such a special time of joy for me with their celebration of giving, sharing, love, happiness, delight, and oneness with God. But for the last twelve years there has also always been a bit of sadness underneath it all. It was twelve years ago that I lost my Mom to cancer. I miss my Mom especially during this time of the year. She was still young when she passed on to Heaven. She was only fifty five years old and I was only twenty five years old when she died. I know that I was blessed with many more years than some children get with their parents, but it still seemed far too soon for her to go. I had barely outgrown the selfishness of my adolescent years and truly begun to appreciate all the love and caring she had given me in my life when the cancer came.

The last four years of her life were the hardest ones and yet they were filled with so much love, joy, goodness, laughter, closeness, and caring. I can remember calling her everyday and ending each phone call with "I love you Mom." We both knew how precious time was by then and we made the most of the time we had left together. I truly do wish, though, that I could hug her one more time, look into her shining eyes and smiling face, and tell her how much I love her.

Losing my Mom when I was so young did teach me one thing: we don't have forever in this world. If we want to share our love and joy with others then we have to do so now. That is why I hug my children everyday, that is why I tell my wife I love her every chance I can, and that is why I write my articles and share my joy with others at every opportunity. Don't let a day go by then without thanking God for your life and sharing your love and joy with everyone you can. Life is short. Live it with love. Live it in joy. I love you Mom.

Tears are a gift from Heaven. They wash away your pain and water the seeds of love in your soul.

BIG BOYS DO CRY

"Big boys don't cry." I heard those words a lot growing up in America in the late sixties and early seventies. In those days men were expected to be tough and rugged and never shed a tear no matter what. Our heros were all stone faced cowboys who were too strong to cry. Believing this then I tried my best never to cry at all during my teenage and early adult years.

All that changed, however, as I was driving home alone one night shortly after my Mom died. It was dark and raining outside. I was struggling to keep the car on the road while at the same time struggling to hold the tears back in my eyes. I remember almost going off the road twice as I blinked back the salty water that was burning my eyes and blurring my vision. My hands shook, my heart hurt, and my soul felt dead. Finally I could do it no longer. I stopped, pulled over, lay my head on the steering wheel, and cried. I cried until the tears couldn't fall anymore. I cried until the pain that I was holding onto so strongly finally fled my heart.

After that night I realized something. Big boys do cry. In fact, it is the biggest hearts that cry the most. I realized too that it is our tears that can release us from our anger and our grief while reconnecting us to our love and our God. Tears help us to embrace this often bittersweet life. They help us to keep growing closer to each other in love and joy instead of shutting ourselves up in dull, aching, and lonely hearts.

These days I cry a lot more often. Sometimes the tears are sad. Sometimes the tears are joyous. But always the tears are full of love. I do my best to follow the advice of Leo Buscaglia who said, "Crying is good! It cleans out your eyeballs!" My eyeballs are a lot cleaner now than they used to be and my heart is as well. I hope then that every boy and girl out there realizes that tears are a gift from Heaven. They wash away the pain and water the seeds of love in your soul.

A little bit of kindness goes a long way.

A KIND LIFE

"A little bit of kindness goes a long way." If there is any phrase that rings true, it is this one. I can remember a few years ago attending the funeral of a friend of mine. We had grown up together, played football and basketball together, attended school together, and in the summer gone to 4-H camp together. We had even worked in the same place as adults for a short time. He was one of the kindest and most fun loving souls I had ever known. He always was willing to help anyone in need. He was always there to offer you a smile, a laugh, and a gentle joke to cheer you up. He was always a source of joy in the lives of everyone who knew him. His kindness, good humor, and happy spirit touched us all.

I can remember the sadness that filled me when I learned that he had died so young. I can remember the heaviness in my heart as I drove to his wake. That heaviness, however, lifted some and a smile came to my face when I saw the line waiting to get into the funeral home. It stretched down the street for as far as I could see. I can remember smiling too when I found out that his funeral had to be held at a local football field to hold all the lives he touched with his kindness and love. That field was later renamed after him. What a fitting tribute to a life that touched so many in such a short time.

The great poet Washington Irving wrote, "A kind heart is a fountain of gladness, making everything in its vicinity freshen into smiles." That was my friend's heart. That was my friend's life. That is why I ask God everyday to fill me with love, joy, and kindness so that I can share them with the world. If I only touch half the souls my friend did then I will consider my life well lived. May all of us live lives of such love and kindness. May all of us touch countless souls with our joy, laughter, light, and oneness with God.

May we never wait in line when it comes to sharing God's love and making the Earth a little more like Heaven.

THE LONGEST LINE

The longest line that I ever stood in wasn't in a store. It wasn't to see a movie or a concert either. It wasn't even in the Department of Motor Vehicles. The longest line I ever stood in was at my friend Tim's wake. Tim had died a young man and his loss had shocked our small community. When I arrived at the wake I was amazed to see the line stretching from inside the small funeral home to down the street as far as the eye could see. People had come from hundreds of miles away to be there and to offer their love to Tim one last time. I saw people there that I hadn't seen since high school and others whom I had thought I'd never see again.

The line moved slowly forward as we waited and shared our memories of Tim. We talked about how funny he had always been without ever seeming mean-spirited once. He loved a good joke and would share them even in a football huddle during the middle of a game. We talked about how Tim was always kind and helpful to anyone in need. In his short but loving life his joyful spirit had touched a thousand people in a thousand different ways. We grieved about how he would never see his kids graduate from school, but also took comfort in knowing that a part of Tim lived on in each of them. We laughed, cried, remembered, and thanked God for the time we had Tim's good soul with us. When his funeral was held later no indoor building could hold it. We had it on the junior high school football field that was later renamed after him.

In his short time here Tim had made his family, our community, and the world so much better. His loss left a hole in us all. Still, I think that we now laugh a little more, love a little deeper, and share joy a bit more often because of how he touched our hearts. Is there any more fitting tribute to a life well lived? May all of us live as well and love as much. May all of us too never wait in line when it comes to sharing God's love and making the Earth a little more like Heaven.

Kai taught me so much about how to be a more loving human being through her words and her life. I couldn't have asked for better knowledge or a greater gift than that.

CAKE WITH KAI

For the last several weeks my oldest son and I have been visiting our neighbor and friend, Kai every Wednesday afternoon. I always bring over my newest bit of writing to share with her and she always greets us with a hug, a smile, and a freshly baked cake. Each week she fills our bellies with another frosted delight. First it was chocolate, then lemon, strawberry, and vanilla. Everyone of them too melts in your mouth and makes your stomach sigh. After cake we all sit down for a long talk full of shared laughs and shared lives.

Kai's name rhymes with Hi and that is fitting because her every greeting is full of love and kindness. It doesn't matter if it is me, the delivery man, or the dog next door. Kai is always ready to give a little joy to everyone she meets. Since she and her husband Sean moved here a few years ago they have made our neighborhood, our community, and our lives so much better. This is all the more amazing considering that the whole time I have known her Kai has been racked by terminal illnesses that have battered every part of her except her spirit.

In the book "Tuesday's With Morrie" author Mitch Albom writes about his visits to an old, college professor who is dying and how much he learned about living from him. I think that my Wednesday afternoons with Kai have done the same for me. Kai has taught me so much about how to be a more loving human being through her words and through her life. I couldn't have asked for better knowledge or a greater gift than that.

I thank God everyday for Kai and Sean and all the wonderful people He has brought into my life over the years. I know too that even after Kai leaves us that we will see her again one day in Paradise. Then there will be plenty of time for sitting, smiles, laughter, love, happiness, hugs, long talks, and perhaps even a piece of cake.

She showed us everyday how to live and how to love, while facing her own coming death.

KAI

My good friend and neighbor, Kai died yesterday. It wasn't unexpected. She had told me in our very first conversation that she had a terminal disease. This week after battling it for several years her body finally gave out. Her soul, however, never did.

Kai was one of those special people who could light up a room just by coming into it. Her full name was Kailani which means Heavenly Sea. It couldn't have been more fitting because she washed over all of us with waves of love. Her dear husband Sean, her family, her friends, her neighbors, her church, and everyone she met was showered with her kindness. She became an adopted grandmother to a neighbor's children. She nursed a dog injured in a bear attack back to health and then adopted it as her own. She helped my daughter make that difficult transition from teenager to adult. She showed me how to be a more open and caring person as well. She invited so many of us into her home and her heart. She fed us cake, told us stories, and gave us the gift of her laughter. She listened to our problems, soothed our fears, and showed us everyday how to live and how to love. And she did it all while facing her own coming death.

In the last talk we had she told me that she hated the fact that she was going to die in the middle of Winter. Well, sometimes God in His love gives me just the right words. I said, "Don't worry Kai, when you awake it will be Spring."

We are going to miss you Kai. We are going to miss that high voice that seemed to sing hello. We are going to miss that gentle smile that warmed our souls. We are going to miss that light you shared that made all of ours burn a little brighter. The tears we are shedding now aren't for you. Your place in Paradise is guaranteed. The tears we are shedding are for us, because we love you. Thank you for coming into our lives and making a forever home in our hearts.

Few things feel better than offering a helping hand to someone in need.

A HELPING HAND

It was the perfect weather for a walk the other day. It was that beautiful time of the year right between the end of Winter and the start of Spring. Cool breezes tickled my face while the rising sun quickly burnt away the morning fog. Birds were starting to sing their love songs again and to built nests for their future young. My heavy coat had been traded for a light jacket. The grass was still moist from the freshly melted snow and the Maples and Oaks seemed to be deep in thought over whether to send out their buds now or wait a few more weeks.

I walked along the edge of the woods and gazed up at the bright, blue sky. As I was thanking God for another glorious morning, however, a sad sound reached my ears. It was a mewing that sounded like a newborn kitten. I looked around on the ground but couldn't see one anywhere. Then I noticed that the crying seemed to be coming from above and glanced up into the trees. I soon spotted him. It was no kitten but a full grown tomcat who had let Spring fever get the best of him. He had scaled an Oak like it was nothing but was now too scared to climb back down.

I knew I couldn't leave him up there but wondered if I would need a ladder to get to him. I decided to let my boyhood tree climbing skills guide me instead. Grasping the rough branches I slowly made my way up to the cat. Then cradling him in one arm I lowered myself down again and safely let him go. He gave me a quick thank you glance and then scurried off. I smiled as I watched him go then headed for home with scraped up hands but a warm heart.

Few things in this life make you feel better than offering a helping hand to someone in need. It connects you with God. It brings you closer to others. It helps you become who you were meant to be. The next time then that you get a chance to give someone a hand up or in the cat's case a hand down take it. A helping hand like a loving heart always leads to a happy soul.

May you write a story that doesn't just end with this life, but goes on to the next.

WHAT ARE YOU GOING TO WRITE?

In the hallway of my son and daughter's high school there is a poster that says: "You are the Author of your own Life Story." This very wise and very true saying made me think of my own life. I have had more rough drafts and editing sessions than I can count, but I think that I am finally writing the story of my life that I always wanted to write. It is a definite best seller when it comes to my soul and that is the only audience any of us should care about.

What kind of story are you going to write? What kind of story are you writing now? Is it a comedy of mistakes and problems that makes you want to laugh and cry at the same time? Is it a tragedy of pain and suffering that you would rather not write at all? Is it a horror story that scares you with every page you turn? Is it a mystery that keeps you guessing what will happen next? Is it a romance that leaves you wishing for a happily ever after ending, but realizing that real life is full of ups and downs? Is it a life affirming triumph of God's love over the troubles in this world that uplifts the heart and soul with every word?

Whatever you choose to write know that you can edit it or rewrite it daily. May I suggest, however, that whatever you write you make it a love story. I am not talking about a typical love story either. I am talking about a love of life story. I am talking about a love of learning and growth story. I am talking about a love of nature, animals, music, and books story. I am talking about a love of laughter, joy, and delight story. Most of all I am talking about a love of yourself, others, and God story. Any story with that much love is bound to be a great read, full of humor, excitement, wisdom, fun, and joy that will touch the heart, mind, and soul. May you write a great story then. May you write a story so good that you never want to put the book down. May you write a story that doesn't just end with this life, but goes on to the next.

It feels so good to use our words to build others up rather than tearing them down.

A FEW GOOD WORDS

I heard the sweetest sound today. It was sweeter than birds singing, wind chimes tinkling, or music playing. It was so beautiful that it instantly made my face smile, my heart sing, and my spirit soar to Heaven. It was my littlest child saying, "I love you."

You know there is nothing like a few good words to make your day and remake your life. Words are such a glorious gift from God. They have the power to spread love, share joy, and create happiness. They have the ability to lift a beaten and battered heart up to the sky. They have the strength to help a despairing soul in its hour of greatest need.

It is a shame then that we don't use more good words in our lives. There is nothing like a few kind words to bring a little goodness and delight into another's life. Mark Twain used to say that he could go for days on a good compliment. It feels so good too when we use our words to build others up rather than tearing them down. It feels so wonderful to share a few honest words of praise. If feels so fantastic to let another person know that they are loved, admired, and cared for.

If you truly want to change your life for the better then make two lists of words. On the first put all the negative words you hear all the time like: hate, hurt, no, can't, pain, destroy, and those I won't even mention here. On the second list put every positive word you can think of like: joy, love, light, delight, peace, happiness, goodness, kindness, fantastic, wonderful, good, great, glorious, and don't forget yes. Then throw away the first list and always use the second. You will be amazed at the miracle that will take place. You will be in awe of the joy, love, peace, and happiness that will flow into your life. You will be filled with wonder at how God, yourself, and a few good words brought Heaven to Earth.

We are all works in progress, but we can still have the time of our lives becoming better for God.

WORKS IN PROGRESS

I snapped at my son today. In a moment of frustration I scolded him over something trivial that I could have easily ignored. I saw the hurt in his eyes after I did it and apologized to him. Afterwards, I gave him a hug, reminded him of what a good son he is, and told him how proud I am of him. Still, I wished I could have taken back what I said earlier.

Later in the day I was in the store getting a few items for dinner. An elderly lady was stretching in vain to reach something on a high self. I walked over and asked if I could help. She said,"Yes" and I got what she needed down for her. She then thanked me for the helping hand and I told her it was my pleasure. I left the store feeling both happier and closer to God.

How do I reconcile that frustrated Father I was earlier in the day with the smiling, good Samaritan I was later in the afternoon? The answer is simple. I am still a work in progress. In truth, we are all works in progress from the second of our birth to the moment of our death. We are here to learn to love, to grow in love, to share our love, and to become one with our Heavenly Father's love. It may seem simple but it isn't always easy. It takes a lifetime too. That is why no matter how many times we stumble and fall it is important to rise up, to ask God's forgiveness, to dust ourselves off, and to begin again to love with all of our heart, soul, mind, and strength. At the end of our lives only one thing matters: how much we loved.

I know that my son will forgive me for my short temper earlier today. I know that God will forgive me too. Like everyone else I still have a lot of work to do to become the person I want to be. Thankfully, God is patient with me. I know too that the job of growing into our goodness can mainly be done with laughter, smiles, and great joy. Yes, we are all works in progress, but we still can have the time of our lives becoming better for God.

Don't forget to LIVE while you make a living.

MAKING A LIVING AND LIVING

The best on the job training I ever got in my life came from a very special woman: my Mom. It happened when I was in my early twenties. I had just recently graduated from college but couldn't find that well paying job I had been hoping for. With a wife and baby son to support at home I found myself reluctantly taking a job as a busboy in a local restaurant. I was bitter, sad, and depressed to find myself working there to say the least.

God works in mysterious ways, though, because that restaurant was the same one that my Mom had recently started working at after years of being a stay at home Mother. The first time I saw her come in the kitchen it was like an extra light had been turned on. Her smile was returned by everyone of the cooks and her gentle laughter and sweet good humor made the shift go by quickly. Her concern for her fellow workers made them open up their hearts to her and she was happy to fill those hearts with her compassion and love. She did her physical work well and did her spiritual work even better. And at the end of the day she seemed to have even more energy than when she had started.

It was both strange and delightful to see my Mom in this new and wonderful way. I had thought that I had learned all that she could teach me, but now I was learning something brand new. Me and most of the other workers at that restaurant were there just to make a living but my Mom was actually LIVING. Her job and her joy had become one. She cooked up love both on the stove and in the hearts of all those around her. She was doing Heaven's work here on Earth.

I have had a lot of jobs since then. Some have been backbreaking and some have been inspiring but I have always tried to follow Mom's example and bring my love and joy to each one. May you do the same and always LIVE while you make a living.

The more love you give the more love you have, and the more love you have the more love you receive.

GIVING, HAVING AND RECEIVING

Love is an amazing thing. It is a glorious gift from God that defies logic, reason, and even explanation. It created the universe, it bonds us all together, and it shines bright in every soul that chooses to share it. The truth is the more love you give the more love you have, and the more love you have the more love you receive.

This truth was made especially clear to me one day last Winter. It was during a spell when each day brought another 8 inches of snow and we wondered if it would ever end. On this day even the heavy snow plows couldn't keep the roads clear. I was on my way to the post office driving 20 mph under the speed limit. It was then that I saw a man and woman hitchhiking on the side of the road. I carefully pulled over and asked where they were going. Although it was an extra 10 miles out of my way I agreed to take them anyway. Traffic was light and I didn't see them catching another ride anytime soon.

As we drove along I learned that they were headed to an elderly friend's home to shovel out her driveway. They had agreed to do so out of the kindness of their hearts, with no thought of reward, and knowing that it would take most of the day to do so and get back home. They thanked me more than once as I dropped them off, but they didn't have to. Their loving example had already touched my heart. It made me smile knowing that my small act of kindness had helped them with their large act of love. Driving back home I felt a wonderful peace and happiness that nothing in this world can give. I felt the powerful, limitless love of God fill my spirit full to overflowing. At that moment I knew what it felt like to live as a true Child of God.

Love truly is what life is all about. It enlightens our souls and encircles our lives here. It connects us to Heaven and makes us one with God. It brings us what we all want: Joy!

Inside of each of us is a child needing love and wanting to be loved.

FEELING LOVED4

I got to hold a baby again recently. I had taken my son to the doctor's office for a checkup and noticed a tired grandmother trying to fill out the office's paperwork and comfort her sick grandchild at the same time. I offered to help and gently rocked the infant back to sleep. With all of my children teenagers now it had been a while since I had held someone quite so small in my arms. As I looked at his sweet, innocent face I couldn't help but to think of what life held in store for him. I knew that it would be a mixture of both joy and fear, laughter and tears, growth and struggle, learning and difficulty, and love and pain. I said a silent prayer that he would learn quickly to choose the good things and not to dwell on the bad. I also prayed that he would always feel loved in this life. I knew that if he felt loved then he would also choose love and share love with so many others as well.

I then said this prayer for the rest of us too. We may be fathers, mothers, and grandparents now, but inside of each of us there is still a child needing love and wanting to be loved. Thankfully, we have a parent who loves us with a love that is both unending and unconditional. We are all Children of God and we are always held in His loving arms as we go through this life. Even if we haven't always felt loved by the people in our lives we can be assured that His love will always be there for us.

May we all feel loved in this life. May we all feel God's love for us from our first breath until our last sigh. May we feel loved through all the joy we experience and through all the pain we must face as well. May we use that love to choose the good things in life and not dwell on the bad. May we use that love to become more loving ourselves every single day of our lives. May we use that love and share our love to help others feel loved as well.

It hasn't been easy walking on the roead of chooseing love and sharing joy, but I wouldn't trade the journey for the whole world. It truly "has made all the difference."

THE ROAD LESS TRAVELED

Like the poet Robert Frost I have been taking the road less traveled for many years now. It has been a twisting and curvy road with many steep hills and rocky spots. It hasn't been well lit or well paved, and I have often stumbled along as I walked it. I have even fallen down time and time again. I have always, however, picked myself back up, dusted myself back off and continued on my way. It hasn't been easy walking on the road of choosing love and sharing joy, but I wouldn't trade the journey for the whole world. It truly "has made all the difference."

This road has strengthened the legs of my soul, exercised the love of my heart, and vitalized the joy in my life. It has taken me to places of beauty and delight that I didn't know existed and has helped me to travel both through the world and into myself at the same time. It has introduced me to the greatest guide and traveling companion imaginable: God, and has helped me to walk in oneness with Him each and everyday of my life.

I have noticed something too. With each day that I walk down the road less traveled, I find more and more beautiful souls walking it as well. With each day I walk down the road of choosing love and sharing joy, I find more and more fellow travelers who have left the more traveled road and followed their hearts and souls to this one.

Don't be afraid to take the road less traveled then. Don't be afraid to take the road of choosing love and sharing joy. The trip may be bumpy and rough at times, but it will always lead you where you need to go. The road may not be as crowded or well lit but with God by your side and beautiful souls walking it with you, it will always be a delight to travel all through this life and on into the next.